W9-CFA-821

NO SHIT, THERE I WAS...AGAIN!

more wild stories from wild people

By Michael Hodgson

Contributing Editor

Illustrations by Dave Sanders

ICS BOOKS, Inc. Merrillville, Indiana

NO SHIT, THERE I WAS... AGAIN!
Copyright © 1995 by Michael Hodgson
10 9 8 7 6 5 4 3 2 1

All rights reserved, including the right to reproduce this book or portions
thereof in any form or by any means, electronic or mechanical, including
photocopying, recording, unless authorization is obtained, in writing, from
the publisher. All inquiries should be addressed to ICS Books, Inc., 1370
East 86th Place, Merrillville, Indiana 46410.

Published by:
ICS BOOKS, Inc.
1370 E. 86th Place
Merrillville, IN 46410
800-541-7323

Co-Published in Canada by:
Vanwell Publishing LTD
1Northrup Crescent
St. Catharines, Ontario L2m 6P5
800-661-6136

All ICS titles are printed on 50% recycled paper from
pre-consumer waste. All sheets are processed without
using acid.

LIBRARY OF CONGRESS CATALOGING-IN-PUBLICATION DATA

No shit! There I was--again / edited by Michael Hodgson.
    p.   cm.
ISBN 1-57034-031-5
1. Adventure and adventures. I. Hodgson, Michael .
G525 . N542   1995
910 . 4--dc20   95-24427
                                     CIP

Table of Contents

Introduction

Any outdoorsperson, armchair or otherwise, has learned that tall tales are the stuff legends are made of, the meat of glory and the marrow of adventure. For centuries, while gathered around campfires or smoky watering holes that smell of beer and musty wood, adventurers the world over have regaled all who will listen in that time-honored tradition of recounting unbelievable stories that more often than not begin with, "No shit! There I Was ... " or some other reasonable facsimile. Exaggeration within moderation is the key. Humor becomes important, although not essential. Elements of the unbelievable are a must.

I must have heard nearly a million such stories during all the years I have spent outdoors—both as a professional guide and an outdoor writer. A number of these stories get handed down from storyteller to storyteller. An even greater number are pure originals, gaining notoriety as much for the teller's art of verbally recounting the event with humor and skill as for the event itself.

Truly great taletellers have the rare ability to make mountains out of molehills, if you give them half a chance. There is a craft in managing to embellish simple cowardice and elevate the tale to recounting an experience of inspiration, valor and glory. A mere sprained ankle on a weekend backpack can turn into an epic event of biblical proportions, bringing smiles and head shakes of disbelief from the listeners when the lips of the skilled spinner of yarns crafts the tale. Yet, too many of these narrations never get shared beyond the realm of the campsite—disappearing come morning like the dying embers of an evening's fire that once coaxed forth story after story.

It is with the above in mind that I set out to begin placing some of these adventure narratives between the covers of a book for all to enjoy—day in and day out. ICS Books and I created a writing contest, seeking the very best "No Shit, There I Was..." accounts the outdoor world was willing to share. Stories arrived from all parts of the country and before long, we had a best-selling anthology on our hands. More stories kept arriving and the floodgates were open. "No Shit" would become an annual writing contest, judged by professionals in the craft of writing and storytelling.

This year's contest received hundreds of entries from which only the best were selected to appear before the judges' panel. I selected the top 23 of these for publication, some from professional writers, some not, all of which now appear in the following pages, published for your enjoyment. For obvious reasons, my two stories which are included in this book were not entered into the contest—had I won, could you imagine the scandal? That would be a "No Shit" story in itself.

My congratulations to this year's "No Shit" grand prize and runner-up winner John Long. John won the grand prize last year as well ... which could lead you to say that either John writes very well or he is just full of _____ . I prefer to believe it is John's talent as a writer and storyteller which vaults him consistently to the top and has made him a best-selling author around the world. I am sure that everyone will have a favorite tale or two tucked in between the pages within. I know I've got mine, and I read them over and over, as I am sure you will, too.

In the meantime, maybe you've got a tale to tell? I hope so, because as you are reading this, ICS Books and I are already seeking and receiving more tales of unbelievable proportions for the next edition of this wonderfully entertaining collection of anthologies, "No Shit, There I Was ..." Continued!

Read on and enjoy. Then, if you do have a tale to share and think you have the right stuff to make it into these pages for storytelling posterity, read the contest criteria in the back of the book and send away for your official entry form.

$1,250 GRAND PRIZE WINNER OF THE 2ND
"NO SHIT, THERE I WAS..." WRITING CONTEST

My Friend Phil

By: John Long

For a dozen years after his solo ascent of Gurishankar, the adventure community was divided into two camps: those who had been with Phil and those who had not. Then during the spring monsoon, he and his two kayaking partners, Marty Silverman and Rick Navarro, paddled into Uruguay's Rio Caiman and were never seen again. That left the rest of us staring at nowhere in particular, unable to appreciate the distance that the river had carried Phil away from us. It didn't seem sad, but impossible. Dozens of articles and several books stoked the memories, as though if we blew hard enough on the embers, the live flame would leap out and again light up the mountains, rivers and caves. Eventually the whole business took on a sort of majesty, until finally his death became more his survivors' affair than his own. This seemed vulgar in a way, though less so than letting him die completely. But time will do what the river never could, and someday I'll forget that Phil and I ever took that Air Nairobi flight, when a terrified stewardess discovered a death adder under a rear seat, and Phil killed it with the fire extinguisher and was marked a hero because only I knew that the goddamn snake had escaped from Phil's own carry-on bag. And I'll probably forget how we took the wrong tributary of the Kasai and were whisked into Angola and

1

the middle of a civil war. And I'd pay money to forget the Solomon Islands and the talking skeleton. We both knew it was bogus but we couldn't expose the stunt; I still hear its toothy jabbering in my sleep. One day I will forget all of these things—but never that first trip to Baja, years before the world had ever heard of Philip Randolph Davenport.

The Davenport family was from another planet, or so thought my father, an Aspen carpenter who had built the deck on the Davenports' summer home near Ajax Mountain. The home, a palatial lodge set on a hillside overlooking Golden Butte, was a curious amalgam of Manhattan chic and aboriginal Peru, and suggested the eccentric union of the Davenports themselves.

Herbert Davenport was something of a kook, a gentleman anthropologist who had fooled nearly 20 years away "studying" antique cultures deep in the Peruvian rain forest. Katherine Putnam Davenport was a 24-carat virago with a tongue like a carving knife. She was the kind that didn't go out in the sun without an umbrella. Her husband had been so long out of circulation that when he returned to the States from the jungle, he was no more fit for any legitimate work than he was for the presidency of the United States. Katherine's tacit agreement with the Davenport patriarchs was that so long as she kept her husband out West, where he couldn't embarrass anyone, their annual allowance of the enormous family fortune was secure.

For more than 15 years, Katherine and Herbert had seen one another only at Christmas and for a few weeks each summer. When phlebitis finally drove Herbert from the rain forest for good (along with Philip, who had spent most of his childhood with his father in Peru), he and Katherine were like strangers thrown together. But Herbert was adrift in the civilized world without his wife's direction, and she was hopeless without his money. For the first year they tolerated each other in a curiously detached way. After another year, they were an inseparable odd couple.

The Davenports spent their summers in Aspen, where Philip and I had both been in my uncle's Explorer Scout troop and fell in together. When the family invited me to join them for a week at their casita near La Paz, Baja California, my folks thought it a workable plan, since I was nearly 16 and had never left Colorado. Philip had a wild streak, and his folks were from Mars, but for all of that they were respectable and monied, and if anything should happen, Dad reckoned they could get me back to Aspen in one piece.

The casita belonged to Herbert's brother, Harold, who had spent a bundle trimming it out, and used it once every couple of years or not at all. A couple hundred yards below the paved road leading to La Paz, and close by the sea, lay a hard-packed dirt road crowded with dog carts, kids on rusty bicycles, women with black rebozos pulled over their shoulders dragging wailing infants by the hand, and peons with great loads of firewood on their bare shoulders trudging toward the charcoal factory in town. Just off this dirt road, set back in a copse of green bamboo, was the casita—a diamond in the rough if ever I saw one.

Set up on creaky oak pylons, the three-bedroom house cantilevered over gulf waters famous for sportfishing. The exterior was plain, but the inside was fitted out for proto-Mexican gentry, with portraits of Cantinflas and Pedro Infante and a few San Sebastian bullfighters on the reed walls; silver-trimmed wicker furniture covered with combed steer hides on the wooden floor; and a collection of pricey Spanish glassware and Toltec artifacts displayed in cabinets against the den walls. A silver horseshoe hung over the kitchen door for luck.

Katherine Davenport hated the place from the moment we arrived. Never mind the decor: ruffians prowled the dirt road just beyond the front door, the electricity was off and on, mostly off, the humidity was terminal, and the flooring was so warped you could see the anxious ocean through the gaps.

On the second night, when Phil and I were swinging face down in hammocks and trying to spit through rifts in the floor, Mrs. Davenport let out a scream that could have frozen mescal. A cucaracha the size of a taquito had scampered across her bedspread, and several fiddler crabs had made their way into the bedroom as well. She swore she wouldn't stay in that house one second longer. Pop Davenport loaded up the rental Jeep and took his wife to the Hotel Hidalgo, a five-star lodging in town. We could come if we wanted to. We didn't. Pop Davenport promised he would swing by in the morning to take us out for breakfast. The Jeep wheeled off, and we were alone.

Philip rifled the liquor cabinet and came away with a black earthenware jug with a cork sealed with melted wax. "The genuine article," Phil said, drawing out the cork with his buck teeth and swallowing enough to shudder his frame, though he forced a smile because he was like that. We moved to the back of the house where a warped plank staircase descended between two rotting pylons from the den straight into the sea. At the bottom step, tied off to one of the pylons, was a frail-looking dinghy. We sat on the last step with our legs in saltwater and gazed out over the moon-rinsed gulf, talking about climbing the Maroon Bells back in Aspen, and maybe doing some bull riding here in La Paz—if we could find a bull. The tequila burned all the way down to our toes; and after the second gulp, I went to the bathroom to check the enamel on my teeth.

The bottle was only a fourth gone when we spotted a giant cutlass carving through the water, flashing like mother-of-pearl as it swiveled into the moonlight. "Shark," Philip whispered.

I bounded up a couple of stairs to a pylon as Philip jumped into the dinghy, snatched an oar and started bashing the water. "Frenzied movements attract them," Philip cried, beating away. "I read it in Argosy."

"Attracts them?" I yelled, clinging to the pylon. "Jesus, Phil. That fin's big as a STOP sign. You sure you wanna be fuckin' with it?" Phil thrashed the water even harder. I moved to the top step as the fin swept close by the dinghy, circled under the house and plowed back into the deep. Philip jumped from the dinghy, splashed up the stairs and into the house, then returned with the remains of our chicken dinner, chumming the water with bones and necks and gizzards. Several times the gleaming fin cruised past but never as close as the first time.

"Blood," Philip said angrily. "We need blood." And he hurled the tequila bottle into the sea.

It was nearly dawn before I could drift off in my hammock, picturing that great fin circling under the bedroom floor. When I woke the next morning, I found Philip in the kitchen, studying the big silver horseshoe hanging above the door. Pop Davenport had already come and gone, and Philip showed me a fat wad of peso notes to prove it. His mom had a fever and his father didn't want to leave her alone in the hotel. We would have to fetch our own breakfast.

Philip reached up above the doorjamb and yanked the horseshoe free from its nails, his eyes burning. "We're going fishing, Jim."

We jogged up to the main road, swung up onto an autobus and were soon scudding around central La Paz, grabbing a cocktail de camarones in one stall, ogling the senoritas in others. In a back alley we found an old man, hunched over a foot-powered grinder, who milled one end of the silver horseshoe into a pick, sharp as fate. I watched the fury of peso notes changing hands, Philip rattling off espanol like a native. Smoking lung-busting Delicados, sin filtros, we hustled on through the fish market, ankle deep in mullet offal. At another stall a fleshy woman, her cavernous cleavage dusted with talc, cut 10 feet of thick chain off a gigantic, rusty spool. "For leader," Philip explained, grabbing my arm and racing off. From another lady in a booth hung with crocheted murals of Jesus Cristo, Philip bought 200 yards of 500-kilo-test polypropylene rope. Meanwhile, her husband welded the chain leader onto the sharpened horseshoe, sparks from the acetylene torch raining over Jesus like shooting stars.

"Now for the bait."

We took a cab to the slaughterhouse on the edge of town. Outside the reeking, sheet-metal structure, Philip waved through a curtain of flies and stopped an Indian girl, maybe 16. Her hair was pulled back in thick black braids to bare a face so striking that armadillos raced up my spine just looking at her. She was selling fried pork rinds and sweetbread, and when Philip asked her a probing question, she killed him with her eyes. Philip cajoled her some more. I couldn't understand a word of their machine-gun Spanish. Slowly, the girl's glare melted into a snigger. When Phil's hand went out with a 10-peso note, she reached for it quick as a frog's tongue. But not quick enough. Philip shook his head, flashing that wily smile of his and holding the bill out of reach. She answered his smile with a sly one of her own, glanced around at empty streets, then quickly hiked up her white muslin blouse, and for about one thousandth of a second my eyes feasted on two perfect brown globes crowned with two perky, pinto bean-like nipples. Then her shirt was back down and the bill was gone from Philip's hand and she was two golden heels hot-footing to some shady nook to admire the gringo boy's money.

"I'd marry her in a second," Phil said, "if I was old enough."

We took a bus back to the casita, laden with a giant bull's heart wrapped in brown paper and twine, and a bucket of red slop so heavy it put my hand to sleep.

On the stairs behind the house, Phil baited the sharpened horse-shoe with the ruby-colored bull's heart, duct-taped a soccer ball to the chain leader just below where he'd tied on the polypropylene rope, then neatly coiled the rope on the stairs and lashed the free end round one of the creaky pylons. As he hefted the bucket of entrails into the dinghy, the armadillos started running over my body again.

"You can either watch the line here in the bow, or row. You pick."

"I thought we were going to just chuck the thing in from here."

"Shark won't go for it. You saw how he shied away last night. And anyway, I bought all this rope."

Two hundred yards of new rope seemed a poor excuse to row into shark-infested waters in a leaky dinghy full of blood and guts; but Phil was already in the boat yelling, "Come on, Jim. It's a two-minute job."

I took the oars and rowed straight out into the gulf, my limbs trembling so horribly I could barely pull. The dinghy was overloaded and tippy as hell, and little geysers spewed up through cracks in the flexing hull. I watched the house slowly recede, the line slithering out from its coil. My chest heaved. The water rose to ankle level around my tennis shoes.

Fifty yards out, Phil tossed the bucket of gore overboard and a dull red ring bled out around us.

"That sucker's any closer than Acapulco, he'll smell this," he said. "Believe it."

"I do."

Phil hurled the big red heart overboard with a plunk, the weight yanking out the chain leader, which chattered over the low gunwale of the dinghy. The soccer ball shot out and sank. Phil panned the flat blue plane for a moment. Then the ball popped up near us, the waters churned and he screamed, "Put your back into it, Jim, or we're goners!"

I heaved at the oars, my heart thundering in my ears and my lungs gasping down mouthfuls of air, the dinghy fairly hydroplaning, Phil bailing with the bucket and screaming, "Pull, man, pull." I pulled harder and faster, trying to retrace the line floating on the water, marking the way back home. The flimsy oars bent horribly as Phil screamed to go faster and faster till my oars were driving like bee's wings. Twenty yards from the house, we were both screaming, breathless and terrified, the dinghy shin deep with water and sinking by the second. A final heave and I powered right into the stairs; the dinghy buckled and split in half, dumping us into carnivorous waters. We splashed and groped for the stairs, then stampeded over each other and through the house and out the front door, puking salt-water and howling, finally collapsing in front of a man selling shaved ice from a pushcart.

Phil lay in the dirt, breathing hard and feigning palsy, his face screwed up and his eyes rolled back in his head. I laughed so hard my stomach felt like it turned inside out.

"Not that we're afraid to die or anything," Phil gasped.

The man with the pushcart couldn't have looked more astonished if he'd seen a burro prance by on its hind legs.

After a few minutes, we stole back into the house, tiptoeing a step at a time through the hall, through the narrow den, past the wall of glassware and artifacts, pausing at the open door and the stairs below and staring out over the gulf at the line sleeping on the surface and the soccer ball bobbing peacefully 50 yards away. There wasn't so much as a crawfish on the line. Never had been.

"Chickenshit shark," Phil mumbled. And we sat down.

For several hours we sat hip to hip on the stairs, gazing out at the bobbing ball so hard that the flat horizon and the heat of high noon put us in a trance. Then everything was quiet. Too quiet.

"Wonder where the gulls went?" I asked.

The rope suddenly jumped out of the water, the staircase groaned and splinters flew off the pylon as the line lashed itself taut as a bowstring.

"He's hooked!" cried Phil.

We leaped up and grabbed the rope as the old pylon bowed against the stairs, rusty nails sprang up from fractured planks and sand crabs scurried out from dark places. Far out on the water we saw an invincible fin, a mad roil of water and a jagged snap. A scythe-shaped tail curled on itself and the rope went slack against the pylon. A gathering surge was tearing straight toward us, looking like a submarine surfacing as the line doubled back on itself. Close to us, the fin swerved suddenly and headed out to open sea. We couldn't appreciate the monster's speed till we noticed the loose line, straightening as fast as if lashed to a cigarette boat.

"Grab the rope, or the house is going with him," Phil yelled, lunging for the line.

There was no checking the creature, but I grabbed the rope because Phil told me to. The shark hit the slack line, wrenched me straight off the stairs and into the playground of the blazing gray terror. I furiously crabbed from the water and up the stairs, and didn't stop running till the den. And there I stood, bloody and wheezing, dripping saltwater onto a 19th-century Malagan rug. I was dry before I staggered back to the stairs.

The line was slack, then taut. Then slack again. We pulled. Phil cursed splendidly. The rope smoked through my raw hands. I wanted to cry. We pulled some more, and Phil continued with his magnificent oaths, dragging forth from earth, heaven and hell the remotest, most colossal, most unheard of conceptions all linked together in a sequence so original, so shocking, so piquant with the odd Spanish word thrown in that I could only stand and pull in complete reverence. It was genius.

After an hour, we'd gained a little. With the rope doubled round a pylon, there was just enough friction that we could lock the beast off—even gain some rope when the tension eased for a second. After two hours, we'd reeled the creature a quarter of the way in. Several times it broke the surface, obsidian eyes glinting in the sun. The line under my hands dripped red, and the saltwater tortured the grooves seared into my palms. The more line we gained, the fiercer the combat. The monster would relax for a moment and we'd win a yard, then the line would twang tight, the pylon would creak, and the stairs would twist and shudder under our feet.

"We need help," Phil said. "Lock that puto off for a minute."

I braced against the pylon and held fast as the house behind me filled with dark-haired boys, street urchins, and even the man with the pushcart, snagged from the dirt road just outside. When the line went momentarily slack, Philip unwound it from the pylon and, racing against time, ran the rope in a straight line from the water up the stairs and through the den, down the hall and right out the front door. The brown crowd turned its back on the casita, each man and boy clasping the rope over the shoulder, Philip yelling, "Hale, hale, hoooooombres." The tug-of-war was on, with "tiburon, tiburon grandote" yelled over and over like a chant at a soccer match.

Philip joined me on the crumbling stairs, hauling hand over hand. Out in the gulf, a huge swell was racing toward us as a shark, big as a four-man bobsled, thrashed against the straining rope.

"Let off," I yelled, releasing the line and backpedaling away. "Tell them to let off."

But it was no good. The gathering crowd was already 50 feet past the front door, their feet churning the dust. Phil and I jumped to a pylon when, with one titanic lurch, they hauled the opalescent monster to light. It flopped bodylong onto the buckling stairs, the silver horseshoe hooked deep through its sawtooth lower jaw, the line taut as a guywire. The beast did a move from the deep, lurched a yard straight up off the stairs and, now airborne, was yanked right past us. Its bear-trap maw snapped and a sandpaper flank rasped the skin off my arm as he jackknifed over the stairs, through the open back door and into the den, a place of leisure and filigreed cabinets, of rum toddies and drowsy vacation afternoons. Another move from 10 fathoms and he clipped the legs out from under the rosewood and ivory table.

"Let off, for Christ's sake," I screamed from the stairs. "Let it go."

But every able man for five miles along the dirt road must have been latched onto that rope, and all 50 of them were hauling for pride and country: cabbies, rummies, men in white suits and wraparound shades, a priest in huaraches, and nine National Guardsmen yelling commands and tapping slackers with batons. But 900 pounds of shark wasn't going easily. A smashing tail, and the cabinets were gone, the Toltec artifacts were so many shards, the Spanish glassware, sand. Colossal teeth shredded filigreed wood, ripped the hides off wicker chairs. A flip and a twirl and he unraveled the Malagan rug. The heaving crowd dragged the monster further through the narrow den. Rich purple blood splattered over bright white walls. A deep-water kip, an airborne nosebutt—and a wall caved in. Salt-rotted wood fractured and floor slats snapped to attention as the ceiling dropped a yard and parted to show a splintered smile of blue Mexican sky.

"Verrrrrga mi friggin' dios de cocksucker from hell!" Phil screamed.

And the brown mob pulled. The great monster died 10 times, then lurched back to life, marking its passage through the open house by knocking Sheetrock off the hallway walls, murdering the grandfather clock and blasting the front door off its hinges.

At last the noble creature lay outside, its hornblende eyes locked on infinity, its jagged mouth open. One of the National Guardsmen probed the cavity with his baton, and in a final show of sea force, the huge mouth snapped shut. The guardsman jumped back with a hickory stub in his hand, yelling, "Hijo de puta!"

For nearly an hour we all stood around in a daze, staring at the great monster as kids prodded it with long sticks and several policemen posed for pictures taken with an antique Kodak Brownie that Philip swore had no film in it.

Word of the conquest spread down the dirt road like a whirlwind, and shortly, a flatbed truck from the fish market sputtered up. The beast was logrolled onto the lift, then into the bed of the truck. In five more minutes, the shark was a relic of memory. The gathered crowd slowly went their way, thumping each other's back, and we were once again alone.

I was grated raw, rope-burned, sunburned, splintered, bloodied and spent, my trunks and shirt in tatters, one tennis shoe gone, my hands two oozing, pulpy knobs. Philip was completely unmarked. His shirt was still tucked in. But the casita couldn't have been more trashed had we trapped a grizzly inside it for two weeks—without food or water.

We tried a hundred different lies on each other but couldn't concoct an excuse as big as that shark. Finally, Philip went to the Hotel Hidalgo to try to explain; and in an example of his transcendental luck, he found his parents preparing to leave on the next plane for the States. His mother thought another night in Mexico might kill her. Without reservations, they were able to secure only two seats on the 4:50 Air Mexicana flight to Los Angeles; but Pop Davenport had booked us on the 6:30 flight that same night. The Davenports would wait for us at the airport in L.A., and we'd all go to Disneyland.

Philip raced back to the casita and, after wandering through the ruins, said, "We've got to torch it."

"Torch it?" I asked.

"Yeah, burn it down."

I pictured myself in a Mexican jail. Forever.

"You want to try and explain this?" Philip laughed, glancing at the ocean through a 10-foot hole in the floor, then up through the rent in the roof. "Gran padre de shit-eating gaffos. This joint's dusted."

"How do we explain the fire?" I asked.

"We don't," Philip smiled. "That's the beauty of it. It burns down after we're gone. And it will."

Philip shagged into town, returned with a cab, a gallon of kerosene, and two votive candles. We threw our suitcases into the cab waiting on the dirt road, then Philip soaked the den floor with the kerosene, planted two candles in the middle of the buckled floor, lit them, walked out the open door and into the cab, and we were off.

As we ground up off the tarmac, we spotted a plume of black smoke out east, rising off the fringe of the ocean. Philip leaned back in his seat and said, "Wonder how long that sucker was?"

When Harold Davenport returned to Mexico two years later, he found two shrimp boats tied up to the blackened pylons where his vacation home had once stood. Nobody seemed to know how the fire had started. Or even when. The casita was simply gone. Just like Phil.

The Green Arch

By: John Long

We came from nowhere towns like Upland, Cucamonga, Ontario and Montclair. None of us had done anything more distinguished than chase down a fly ball or spend a couple of nights in juvenile hall, but we saw rock climbing as a means to change all that. Lonely Challenge, The White Spider, Straight Up—we'd read them all, could recite entire passages by heart. It is impossible to imagine a group more fired up by the romance and glory of the whole climbing business than we were. There was just one minor problem: There were no genuine mountains in Southern California. But there were plenty of rocks. Good ones, too.

Every Saturday morning during the spring of 1972, about a dozen of us would jump into a medley of the finest junkers $200 could buy and blast for the little alpine hamlet of Idyllwild, home of Tahquitz Rock. The last 26 miles to Idyllwild is a twisting road, steep and perilous in spots. More than one exhausted Volkswagen bus or wheezing old Rambler got pushed a little too hard, blew up and was abandoned, the plates stripped off and the driver, laden with rope and pack, thumbing on toward mecca. We had to get to a certain greasy spoon by 8 o'clock, when our little group, the Stonemasters,

13

would meet, discuss an itinerary, wolf down some food and storm off to the crags with all the subtlety of a spring hailstorm.

The air was charged because we were on a roll, our faith and gusto growing with each new climb we bagged. The talk within the climbing community was that we were crazy, or liars, or both; and this sat well with us. We were loudmouthed 18-year-old punks, and proud of it.Tahquitz was one of America's hot climbing spots, with a pageant of pivotal ascents reaching back to when technical climbing first came to the States. America's first 5.8 (The Mechanic's Route) and 5.9 (The Open Book) routes were bagged at Tahquitz, as was the notion and the deed of the "first free ascent," a route first done with aid but later climbed without it (The Piton Pooper, 5.7, circa 1946). John Mendenhall, Chuck Wilts, Mark Powell, Royal Robbins, Tom Frost, TM Herbert, Yvon Chouinard, Bob Kamps and many others had all learned the ropes there.

The Stonemasters arrived on the scene about the same time that the previous generation of local hard cores—a smug, high-blown group of would-be photographers and assistant professors—was being overtaken by house payments and squealing brats. They hated every one of us. We were all 90 cents away from having a buck, ragged as roaches, eating the holes out of doughnuts and we cared nothing for their endorsement. We'd grappled up many of their tougher climbs not with grace, but with pure gumption and fire, and the limelight was panning our way.

The old guard was confounded that we of so little talent and experience should get so far. When it became common knowledge that we were taking a bead on the hallowed Valhalla (one of the first 5.11 routes in America)—often tried, but as yet unrepeated—they showed their teeth. If we so much as dreamed of climbing Valhalla, we'd have to wake up and apologize. The gauntlet was thus thrown down: If they wouldn't hand over the standard, we'd rip it from their hands. When, after another month, we all had climbed Valhalla, some of us several times, the old boys were stunned and saw themselves elbowed out of the opera house by kids who could merely scream. And none could scream louder than Tobin Sorenson, the most conspicuous madman ever to lace up Varappes.

Climbing had never seen the likes of Tobin, and probably never will again. He had the body of a welterweight, a lick of sandy brown hair and the faraway gaze of a born maniac. Yet he lived with all the precocity and innocence of a child. He would never cuss or show the slightest hostility; and around girls, he was so shy he'd flush and stammer. But out on the sharp end of the rope, he was a fiend in human form. Over the previous summer he'd logged an unprecedented string of gigantic falls that should have ended his career, and his life, 10 times over. Yet he shook each fall off and clawed straight back onto the route for another go, and usually got it. He became a world-class climber very quickly because anyone that well formed and savagely motivated gains the top in no time—if he doesn't kill himself first. And yet when we started bagging new climbs and first free ascents, Tobin continued to defy the gods with his electrifying peelers. The exploits of his short life deserve a book. Two books.

One Saturday morning, five or six of us hunkered down in our little restaurant in Idyllwild. Tahquitz was our oyster. We'd pried it open with a piton and for months had gorged at will; but the fare was running thin. Since we had ticked off one after another of the remaining new routes, our options had dwindled to only the most grim or preposterous. During the previous week, Ricky Accomazzo had scoped out the Green Arch, an elegant arc on Tahquitz's southern shoulder. When Ricky mentioned he thought there was an outside chance that this pearl of an aid climb might go free, Tobin looked like the Hound of the Baskervilles that had just heard the word "bone," and we had to lash him to the booth so we could finish our oatmeal.

Since the Green Arch was Ricky's idea, he got the first go at it. Tobin balked, so we tied him off to a stunted pine and Ricky started up. After 50 feet of dicey wall climbing, he gained the arch, which soared above for another 80 feet before curving right and disappearing in a field of big knobs and pockets. If we could only get to those knobs, the remaining 300 feet would go easily and the Green Arch would fall. But the lower corner and the arch above looked bleak. The crack in the back of the arch was too thin to accept even fingertips, and both sides of the corner were blank and marble-smooth. But by pasting half his rump on one side of the puny corner, and splaying his feet out on the opposite side, Ricky stuck to the rock—barely—both his arse and his boots steadily oozing off the steep, greasy wall. It was exhausting duty just staying put, and moving up was accomplished in a grueling, precarious sequence of quarter-inch moves. Amazingly, Ricky jackknifed about halfway up the arch before his calves pumped out. He lowered off a bunk piton, and I took a shot.

After an hour of the hardest climbing I'd ever done, I reached a rest hold just below the point where the arch swept out right and melted into that field of knobs. Twenty feet to pay dirt. But those 20 feet didn't look promising.

There were some sucker knobs just above the arch, but those ran out after about 25 feet and would leave a climber in the bleakest no-man's land, with nowhere to go, no chance to climb back right onto the route, no chance to get any protection, and no chance to retreat. We'd have to stick to the arch.

Finally, I underclung about 10 feet out the arch, whacked in a suspect knifeblade piton, clipped the rope in—and fell off. I lowered to the ground, slumped back and didn't rise for 10 minutes. I had weeping strawberries on both ass cheeks and my ankles were rubbery and tweaked from splaying them out on the far wall.

Tobin, unchained from the pine, tied into the lead rope and stormed up the corner like a man fleeing Satan on foot. He battled up to the rest hold, drew a few quick breaths, underclung out to that creaky, buckled, driven-straight-up-into-an-expanding-flake knifeblade, and immediately cranked himself over the arch and started heaving up the line of sucker knobs.

"No!" I screamed up. "Those knobs don't go anywhere!" But it was too late.

Understand that Tobin was a born-again Christian, that he'd smuggled Bibles into Bulgaria risking 25 years on a Balkan rock pile, that he'd studied God at a fundamentalist university and none of this altered the indisputable fact that he was perfectly mad. Out on the sharp end he not only ignored all consequences, but actually loathed them, doing all kinds of crazy, incomprehensible things to mock them. (The following year, out at Joshua Tree, Tobin followed a difficult, overhanging crack with a rope noosed around his neck.)

Most horrifying was his disastrous capacity to simply charge at a climb pell mell. On straightforward routes, no one was better. But when patience and cunning were required, no one was worse. Climbing, as it were, with blinders on, Tobin would sometimes claw his way into the most grievous jams. When he'd dead-end, with nowhere to go and looking at a Homeric peeler, the full impact of his folly would hit him like a wrecking ball. He would panic, wail, weep openly and do the most ludicrous things. And sure enough, about 25 feet above the arch those sucker knobs ran out, and Tobin had nowhere to go.

To appreciate Tobin's quandary, understand that he was 25 feet above the last piton, which meant he was looking at a 50-foot fall, since a leader falls twice as far as he is above the last piece of protection. The belayer (the man tending the other end of the rope) cannot take in rope during a fall because it happens too fast. He can only secure the rope—lock it off. But the gravest news was that I knew the piton I'd bashed under the roof would not hold a 50-foot whopper. On really gigantic falls, the top piece often rips out, but the fall is broken sufficiently with a lower piece to stop you. In Tobin's case, the next lower piece was some dozen feet below the top one, at the rest hold, so in fact, Tobin was looking at close to an 80-footer— maybe more with rope stretch.

As Tobin wobbled far overhead, who should lumber up to our little group but his very father, a minister, a quiet, retiring, imperturbable gentleman who hacked and huffed from his long march up to the cliffside. After hearing so much about climbing from Tobin, he'd finally come to see his son in action. He couldn't have shown up at a worse time. It was like a page from a B-movie script, us cringing and digging in, waiting for the bomb to drop; the good pastor, wheezing through his mustache, sweat-soaked and confused, squinting up at the fruit of his loins; and Tobin, knees knocking like castanets, sobbing pitifully and looking to plunge off at any second.

There is always something you can do, even in the grimmest situation, if only you keep your nerve. But Tobin was gone, totally gone, so mastered by terror that he seemed willing to die to be rid of it. He glanced down. His face was a study. Suddenly he screamed, "Watch me! I'm gonna jump."

We didn't immediately understand what he meant.

"Jump off?" Richard wanted to know.

"Yes!" Tobin wailed.

"NO!" we all screamed in unison.

"You can do it, son!" the pastor put in.

Pop was just trying to put a good face on it, God bless him, but his was the worst possible advice because there was no way Tobin could do it. Or anybody could do it. There were no holds! But inspired by his father's urging, Tobin reached out for those knobs so very far to his right, now lunging, now hopelessly pawing the air.

And then he was off. The top piton shot out, and Tobin shot off into the grandest fall I've ever seen a climber take and walk away from—a spectacular, tumbling whistler. His arms flailed like a rag doll's and his scream could have frozen brandy. Luckily, the lower piton held and he finally jolted onto the rope, hanging upside down and moaning softly. We slowly lowered him off and he lay motionless on the ground and nobody moved or spoke or even breathed. You could have heard a pine needle hit the deck. Tobin was peppered with abrasions and had a lump the size of a pot roast over one eye. He lay dead still for a moment longer, then wobbled to his feet and shuddered like an old cur crawling from a creek. "I'll get it next time," he grumbled.

"There ain't gonna be no next time!" said Richard.

"Give the boy a chance," the pastor threw in, thumping Tobin on the back.

When a father can watch his son pitch 80 feet down a vertical cliff, and straightaway argue that we were shortchanging the boy by not letting him climb back up and have a second chance at an even longer whistler, we knew the man was mad, and that there was no reasoning with him. But the fall had taken the air out of the whole venture, and we were through for the day. The "next time" came four years later. In one of the most famous leads of that era, Ricky flashed the entire Green Arch on his first try. Tobin and I followed.

Tobin would go on to solo the north face of the Matterhorn, the Walker Spur and the Shroud on the Grandes Jorasses (all in Levi's), would make the first alpine ascent of the Harlin Direct on the Eiger, the first ascent of the Super Couloir on the Dru, would repeat the hardest free climbs and big walls in Yosemite, and would sink his teeth into the Himalaya. He was arguably the world's most versatile climber during the late 1970s. But nothing really changed: He always climbed as if time were too short for him, pumping all the disquietude, anxiety and nervous waste of a normal year into each route.

I've seen a bit of the world since those early days at Tahquitz, have done my share of crazy things, and have seen humanity with all the bark on, primal and raw. But I've never since experienced the electricity of watching Tobin out there on the very quick of the long plank, clawing for the promised land. He finally found it in 1980, attempting a solo winter ascent of Mount Alberta's north face. His death was a tragedy, of course. Yet I sometimes wonder if God Himself could no longer bear the strain of watching Tobin wobbling and lunging way out there on the sharp end of the rope, and finally just drew him into the fold.

Iditamania

By: Michael Hodgson

As my plane touched down, the sun's rays still probed the snow-covered expanse, creating a deceptive image of warmth in a region landlocked by ice. I was in Alaska as one of a handful of journalists who had managed to obtain coveted VIP press credentials for the finish of the 1994 Iditarod in Nome. In eager pursuit of adventure, I raced out of the plane and ... aiiieyeargggg! My feet desperately tried to remain under my body, executing what someone told me later was a most excellent rendition of the boot-scoot-and-boogie on ice while my arms churned in the air grabbing for handholds that didn't exist. Within seconds, I lay spread-eagled on the tarmac, gazing at a beautiful Alaska evening sky, my press pass flapping proudly in the breeze, proclaiming to all that VIP stood for Very Inept Person. This was not a good beginning.

I made it to my hotel room without further incident, quite possibly because everyone seemed to be going out of their way to help me stay on my feet. At least I knew that Nome was a friendly place. Not wanting to waste a minute of time, I quickly dressed in the official musher's gear that Timberland had so graciously offered me. As I disappeared into the folds of fabric that belonged to an anorak parka big enough to keep the city of Anchorage warm, I began to get a very bad feeling. Getting lost in one's own clothing is not

21

considered good form even in the most tolerant of circles; but there I was, wriggling and cursing while trying to figure out where my hands and head should go. You would think that something this big would come with a map and perhaps a night-light for guidance purposes.

"Martin Buser is just over an hour out," said a somewhat detached voice from somewhere near the door.

I wriggled a bit more and managed to push the hood out of my face so I could view the man behind the voice. Realizing my struggle with the anorak had an audience and that I had managed to put the damn thing on backward, I was left with no alternative but to grin sheepishly and comment, "We don't usually have to wear this much clothing in California ... hah hah ...."

"I can see that," he said fighting back obvious hysteria. What he really meant was: *"Sheesh, what a complete dweeb. It's a wonder that he can even tie his own shoes."*

Feeling a bit like a cross between the Michelin Man and the Pillsbury Dough Boy, I waddled across the room and followed my escort to the burled wood arch that marked the finish line. Flags and sponsorship banners flapped in the wind as hundreds of spectators, some dressed only in short sleeves and baseball caps, already thronged the restraining fence. I stood in the middle of the chute staring at these half-dressed people, obviously inebriated beyond comprehension, wondering how soon it would be until body parts began breaking off in the subzero cold. Now that would be a story. Apparently, the level of warmth locals felt was directly proportional to the quantity, though not the quality, of 9-billion proof antifreeze coursing through their veins.

The warning siren went off, the traditional announcement that a musher had reached the edge of town and was minutes away from the chute. Like a stream of lemmings, spectators flooded out of the several restaurants, bars and hotels lining Main Street. This routine repeated itself almost hourly, day or night for the next three days. Apparently, no one sleeps in Nome.

Not to belittle the race excitement, but once you've seen several dog teams pant their way into town, you've pretty much covered the finish line angle. I needed more to get the full flavor of my Iditarod experience. Fortunately, the race officials and the town dignitaries did their level best to keep me fed with adventure opportunity. They even offered me the use of the mayor's official vehicle, which I used to check out life at a remote race checkpoint.

While en route, the vehicle's police scanner crackled, "Ahh, Bob ... have you seen Bert's truck while you were out on patrol?"

"That's negative, Marty ... you mean Bert's lost it again?"

"10-4, Bob. We've checked his house and his neighbors but didn't find the truck. Apparently he parked it outside the Bering Sea (a bar); and when he came out later, it wasn't there."

"I copy. Are you sure no one borrowed it?"

"Affirmative ... it looks as if someone might have stolen the truck."

"10-4 ... I'll keep my eyes open."

After a few minutes, the radio crackled again. "Ahh, Bob?"

"Copy, Marty ... what you got?"

"Bert found his truck ... it was parked outside the Nugget Inn (another bar)."

Love it. Only in Nome during the Iditarod could a local park his car in front of one bar and then forget that the bar he was now in was not the bar where he started drinking two doors down. I have to remember to thank the mayor for the use of his scanner. As for the checkpoint, there were dogs, it was cold, and the night was dark. I needed more.

Back at the race headquarters, I met up with another journalist, John, and asked him what one did in this town for fun at 3 a.m.. He grinned and said, "Let's start with a round of tequila shots like you've never had."

Never one to turn down an opportunity for a rollicking good time, especially when a story might go along with it, I dutifully followed my "guide" into the bar and past a crowd of men and women all having what seemed to be too much of a good time. There, belly up to the bar, I got my first inkling of what John meant by "tequila shots like you've never had."

Bertha, the bartender, was a rotund, big-breasted woman. How anyone could manage to fit that much woman into what couldn't have been more than a size 10 T-shirt and pants was beyond me. In fact, the seams of her shirt and pants were being stressed beyond the designer's load limits, I'm sure, and were in danger of exploding and releasing Bertha in all directions. It was not a pretty sight. Bertha smiled a gap-toothed grin and smacked two shot glasses down on the bar in front of her, along with a shaker of salt and a bowl of limes.

I was getting a very bad feeling about this. She topped each tumbler and then turned to John with a twinkle in her brown eyes and asked if he was ready. Before he could answer, Bertha did the unthinkable. Grabbing her shirt, she lifted forcefully and unleashed her breasts onto the bar where they slapped down with a resounding whack that brought back memories of wet towel fights in the boys' locker room. The crowd in the bar went wild. John squeezed, sprinkled, licked and drank. The crowd roared its approval and then John turned expectantly to me.

The idea of placing my tongue on unwashed breasts that were larger than the Texas Panhandle and still jiggling like Bill Cosby's worst Jell-O commercial nightmare was, well, more than my stomach could handle. My lips went very dry and my tongue began to seize up at the mere thought of what I might ask it to do.

I glanced nervously at the crowd and then at John whose grin wrapped at least twice around his face, then back at the mass of flesh still jiggling on the bar. It was the moment of truth. Was I going to muster up the courage to go where I'm sure a million other inebriated men had gone before or was I ... a loud siren sounded, announcing the imminent arrival of another musher. SAVED! The crowd streamed dutifully out the door toward the finish line, sweeping John along with them and leaving me sitting alone with Bertha. I shrugged and beat a hasty retreat for the door without having my drink.

"You can put those away now ... it would have been fun, but I've got work to do and a story to cover ... maybe later." Later. Yeah, like when hell freezes over. I wonder if Bertha was disappointed.

As the sun rose over the frozen ground, I found myself sitting in the front seat of an observation plane. The pilot had instructions to fly me along the race route to White Mountain checkpoint and then back. Hopefully, we would see dog teams on the trail and get some good photos. The air was cold and crisp as we skidded to a stop on the White Mountain airport runway. In short order, the White Mountain "limo service" arrived—a snowmobile pulling an open and very rickety toboggan.

I got in and my elderly Eskimo driver gunned the throttle. Within seconds, I was airborne, getting an impromptu tour of the entire toboggan, front to back. Periodically, I slammed back to earth, leaving just enough time to relocate my teeth and other miscellaneous body parts before being launched skyward again. Somehow my primordial instincts willed my buttocks to clench with all their might on the single rib running the length of the toboggan. It was skill I never imagined I would need, but now used gratefully to anchor my rear end firmly. If I had a tail, I would have wrapped it around something, too, probably my driver's neck. Snow spray settled finely over me as the craft sideswiped to a power-slide stop in front of the race checkpoint.

An hour later, having survived one more toboggan trip with the "maniac Eskimo from hell," I sat gratefully in the observation plane's padded seat. The wind on the ground had picked up and was whipping the surface-snow into a miniblizzard as we took off. The theme to Gilligan's Island came to mind as our tiny plane lurched on the airwaves like a bucking bronco.

The pilot nodded off to the right to draw my attention to several dog teams racing down the track into a wooded area.

"That would make a great photo ... want me to bank the plane?"

I nodded, not entirely sure that I did. The plane banked, the wind blew and suddenly we were flying in a manner that seemed to defy all known laws of aerodynamics and gravity.

"Did you get the shot?" Apparently, being tossed about in the sky like a piece of lint in a Laundromat dryer was all in a day's work for him.

"Ahhh, no, but that's okay, really ... it's no problem." Actually, I would have loved to have had the shot, but there was no way I was going to physically pry my fingers off the plane's instrument panel long enough to steady my camera. Now, how far away was the Nome Airport, and where in the heck were those airsick bags?

Back on terra firma, my thoughts drifted to dogs. I felt the urge to mush. No sooner had I voiced my desire than there I was, standing on the back of a sled's runners with an eager team of dogs yipping and prancing in front of me. After a 30-second how-to-drive-a-dog-team tutorial, I yelled, "Mush," and we rocketed onto the training track at a bajillion miles per hour. I was free-solo in command of the team while a snowmobile shadowed nearby for safety and to pick up the pieces if needed.

The first corner zoomed closer as the team jetted downhill. My mind raced as I tried to remember, was it "gee" for right or "haw?" Crossing my fingers, I screamed, "Gee," and the team swept right around the turn. Whooyaa! I was a musher, lord of the snow and master of all manly sports. That is until the team whipped the sled through a couple of short snake turns and a riotous whoopdeedoo.

Somewhere in the middle of the bouncing, my feet became detached from the runners. The sled tipped and the lead dog looked over his shoulder as if to say, "Guys, a few more of those and we can dust this rookie." Not that I'm overly sensitive, but I took exception to that dog sneering at me. With a lunge and an acrobatic vault, I hurled the sled back upright and clung desperately to the handles while trying to tap dance my feet back onto sled runners that were flying like a runaway train. My mother will be glad to know that all of those dance classes she forced me to take when I was little finally came in use because I Texas two-stepped, rumbaed, Charlestoned, waltzed, tangoed, and even soft-shoed all around and finally onto the bouncing runners, much to my lead dog's chagrin. Back at the finish line, I collapsed, exhausted and drenched in sweat, but still attached to my sled. My newfound friends were doubled up on the snow with laughter. There is little doubt that all three dogs in my team snickered at me all the way back to the kennel.

After just a few days and nights, I had made such an impression in Nome that it was rumored the race officials were thinking of headlining me as next year's entertainment. One thing is for certain. Anyone who visits here needs to pack a good sense of humor and watch where they step, 'cause Nome goes to the dogs in March. Oh, one last tip ... don't eat the yellow snow.

Old Rocksalt and the Whopper in the Bay

By: Michael Shepherd

No shit! There I was … again! Old Rocksalt was the meanest, sneakiest, shotgun totin'est ol' fart I'd ever had the bad luck to have chasing my butt. And there I was again, sneaking onto his land to go fishing at the Secret Spot.

Old Riley Trippett owned a half-mile wide, three-mile long swath of wetlands that separated the water of San Francisco's East Bay from the township of San Lorenzo, a small suburb nestled between the cities of San Leandro and Hayward. When the lowlands and creeks flooded in the rainy season, plenty of grazing land remained for his 80 head of cattle to wander about on. The land held plenty of pheasant, jackrabbit and ground squirrel. There were thick flocks of sandpipers and other shorebirds out there, and white cattle egrets often spotted the grasslands and creeks.

Duck, geese, cormorants and coot bobbed upon the water off the long shore of broken concrete slabs and boulders. Beneath the floating fowl, lurked sturgeon, sand sharks and leopard sharks, stingray, halibut and stripers, when they were running, along with a variety of smaller fish. At low tide, long mudflats were exposed, which gave people the idea that the fishing wasn't any good out there. If you didn't know where to go; it usually wasn't. A small number of us local boys did know where to go, but after several trespassers over the years, myself included, had our backsides blasted with screaming-hot rocksalt from Riley Trippett's shotgun, no one but the most daring and foolish went fishing out there anymore. At 18, I was all of that.

I don't believe Old Rocksalt was born mean. I think he got that way from decades of dealing with dirt-bike riders ripping across his land and chasing his cattle all over the place. And from those KNOT-HEADS that used to go out there and shoot any critter they could get a bead on—including Trippett's cattle. Crazy ol' Billy Hyde had been one o' those knot-heads; he shot it out with ol' Trippett and got himself killed out there, but peppered-up the ol' guy real good before croakin'. A clear case of justifiable homicide, the authorities ruled, but jeez, that goes to show ya just HOW tough that scrawny ol' coot could be!

He wouldn't "normally" shoot you with lead unless you aimed, or shot at him or his cattle first. But he WOULD light your hide on fire with his special-loaded rocksalt shells, if he caught you out there on his land. Aw, if he wanted to kill ya, he could have. He'd let you get far enough away so the rocksalt loads wouldn't kill ya. But let me tell you, I KNOW, you'd still be a bleeding, burning mess; running, stumbling and crawling to get away. And the pain? You-don't-ever-want-to-find-out.

You might go out several times and never see Old Rocksalt once. Then one day you'd see his ol' rattly bang truck racing out after you, or he'd just pop-up out of a creek bed, or someplace, and start shooting and yelling. Scared the living CRAP out of ya when he did that! And there I was again. Trespassing. Sneaking onto Trippett's land to fish that irresistibly good fishing hole where the big creek pours into the bay: the Secret Spot.

It was a half hour before dawn when I pulled my Chevy Fleetside into the back parking lot of the San Lorenzo Community Center's park. I grabbed my knapsack and pole, and walked the 30 yards to the cyclone fence that divided the park and community from the wetlands. I listened and peered out for a moment at the starlit expanse of land, then quietly climbed over where the mashed-down corner of the cyclone fence met the Larkin's redwood backyard fence. A straight shot of railroad tracks paralleled the line of residential, park and golf course fences in both directions. I crunched over the mound of railroad rocks and track, then picked my way through the 4-foot, barbed-wire fence. I was now on Old Rocksalt's land.

I squatted down and scanned the land, looking for the outline of anyone moving out there. It appeared to be clear of both people and cattle, so I headed out, angling right, toward the cover of a small creek. I followed that a ways, then had to cut left, diagonally across a flat expanse of open, patchy grassland. A killdeer's frantic whistle pierced the night close by, and I squatted down again to check my surroundings. Ya just never knew with Old Rocksalt. All was quiet and still, so I resumed my hike.

Dawn lightened the sky as I reached the levee that protected the land from the bay. I went over that and worked my way along the rocks southward, keeping out of sight below the top of the levee. The water was calm and the morning was being born so clear that I could almost reach out and touch the seven-mile long San Mateo Bridge and the cities across the bay. It wasn't high tide yet, so I was doing OK, timewise. The Spot was about a mile farther, and not far from Old Rocksalt's house, which was about a quarter mile beyond the Spot and inland. And that was the reason not too many fellers fished out there. It was just too close.

When I reached the Spot, the April sun was in full view, chasing away the morning chill, and the bay was already alive with birds. The newspaper said the tide would be unusually high this morning, and it was; the creek was filled with saltwater as far back as I could see. The high tide made the creek 30 feet wide and about 6 feet deep at the mouth.

A few dozen yards offshore, a sheet of anchovies surfaced in unison with their mouths and gills gaped and flared, and nipped at the air before disappearing. They resurfaced every few yards, then all of a sudden they came flipping out of the water and skittered every which way in panic—stripers!

I had my dad's 9-foot surf rod already rigged-up with a steel leader and a heavy-duty snapswivel; ya didn't always know what you'd hook into, and sharks were good for biting through mono line. I could see the shadows of stripers moving out of the mouth of the creek toward the ruckus, so I dug a 6-inch Rapala out of my knapsack. That was quicker than the frozen sardines I'd brought along. I slung my first cast to where I last saw the anchovies and no sooner had I started working that lure than whap! Fish on! It peeled line a little too easy, so I tightened the drag a tad and commenced to do battle ...

That first striper was close to 30 pounds, and it felt good hefting that bass up before releasing it. The Spot was as good as ever! I caught 10 more stripers weighing from 15 to 30 pounds each by the time the tide had turned and dropped a couple feet. That first Rapala was wrecked by then, and the bass just weren't taking lures anymore, so I dug out a sardine rig and went with that. I wanted to catch one last striper to take home. I tossed that sardine as far out as I could, and left it alone until it got nibbled off by bait-stealers. I put on another sardine and cast it to another spot, and before I could set the pole in the rocks—WHAP!

That Whopper just about yanked my arm outta the socket! I set the hook real good and the fight was on! That beast pulled so hard that I couldn't stay standing. I planted my butt on a big rock and dug in my heels. Dad liked to keep ridiculously heavy mono line in his reel, some 100-plus test, and now, I was glad of it. The giant striper leapt clear of the water and tried to shake the hook, and my eyes about popped outta my head—that BEAST was all of 5-feet long, and fatter than a prize potbellied pig! A world record striped bass on MY line!

I wasn't about to lose this monster, so I tried not to let it take too much line. I got up and walked out onto the growing mudflat that the receding tide was exposing. It kept taking more line than I could retrieve, so I walked farther out. The Whopper wasn't slowing down and I was starting to worry that I might lose it, so I tightened the drag a little more. It pulled so hard that I had to lean back to keep from being pitched forward. Then the line went slack and I went splat, right on my butt. He'd changed direction, so I sat there and reeled-in a whole bunch of slack. Then ...

BOOM! The shotgun blast kicked up mud right beside me, and I about jumped outta my skin!

"Drop yer pole, pick up yer ass and RUN, you sum'bitch! Run or I'll blast yer trespassin' ass intuh chum!" Clack-clack went Old Rocksalt's pump. He stood atop the levee, a bent, rickety ol' stick man, his huge mustache blowing in the breeze like twin golden flags.

"Don't shoot, Mr. Trippett! I got a world-record bass on the line! Please don't shoot!" I yelled, scrambling to my feet.

"Yer ASS is gonna have a world-record load of rocksalt in it if ya don't drop that pole and bear feet offa my land, boy! I'm countin' tuh three, and ya best be MOVIN'—one, two, three!" BOOM!

The blast hit my side, back and butt, and I fell forward into the stinkin' mud. "Ahhh! Son-of-a-! All right! All right, Mr. Trippett!" Rocksalt eats right through the initial numbness of the blast and quickly begins to ravage your pain sensors. I was in a world of hurt, but I held on tight to my pole. I was NOT going to give up this bass!

I had an idea.

I struggled to get up and tightened the drag all the way. The Whopper ran straight out again and I had to run with it, or let go of the pole. When I started to run, I lost a boot in the muck. The suction pulled it right off my dang foot. By now, I was some 30 or 40 yards from the levee and Old Rocksalt's shotgun.

BOOM! I was hit again, and I stumbled and fell forward into the receding tide. The water was a foot deep and I held onto that pole with both hands. I kicked my feet like a champion swimmer and let that giant bass tow me out, away from that crazy ol' Trippett.

"Ya wanna play smart-ass, you sum'bitch? Ya best keep swimmin' 'cause yer gettin' lead next! If I catch you on my land again, yer gettin' lead! That's all! I know you were a friend o' that Billy Hyde, you sum'bitch! Lead! Ya hear?!" BOOM!

Oh man, I was never a friend of Billy Hyde's, but if that's what Old Rocksalt thought, that's all that mattered in his mind. I kept kicking and that bass kept towing until I was a good 80 yards out. I was in 4 feet of water, that ol' bass was about all done, and I was hurting something terrible. Old Rocksalt was nowhere in sight. I reeled that Whopper in, and yup, he was done. I removed the hook, then I reached down and took off my sock that was half hanging off my foot, and looped it through the striper's huge gill slit and mouth. I tied a strong knot in it, and held that sock firmly in my fist.

Aw man, I hurt. I sure in the heck hoped that no man-eaters had strayed into this end of the bay, like they sometimes do, 'cause I'd lost a smidgen of blood. I waded northward and stayed in the water about 80 yards off the levee. That ornery ol' nut was probably watching.

After a mile or so, I felt safe enough to come out of that bone-chilling water. I hefted that monster over my shoulder, and I'll tell you what, I once worked at Leslie Salt in Fremont, humping 100-pound sacks; I know what 100 pounds feels like, and I had me a striper that beat the world record by better than 20 pounds.

I slogged outta that bay with my trophy catch, a bare foot and a squishy boot, and warily crossed the northern end of Old Rocksalt's land. I was wet, muddy, tired and cold, and in a whole lotta pain. I had to keep shifting that bass from shoulder to shoulder 'cause it was so dang heavy.

Another 100 yards and I'd be home free ...

BOOM! Clack-clack. BOOM! Clack-clack. "Lead! Ah got lead for yer ass, boy!" Yelled ol' Rocksalt. BOOM!

Jeezuss Christ! I sure am glad I didn't have to go number-two 'cause I dang sure mighta went right then. Yes, even that muscle wasn't up to dealing with anymore of Old Rocksalt's surprises. I didn't feel hit, but I could tell he hit my bass. Old Rocksalt wasn't far behind me. I staggered forward and ran the best I could. True to form, that ol' coot had popped-up outta nowhere and got to blasting. BOOM!

I don't recall climbing the barbed wire, crossing the tracks or scrambling over the park's fence, but I do vaguely recall lots of fish guts getting snagged here n' there. I tossed that bass into the back of my truck and drove a couple of blocks before I settled down enough to remember the hot pain in my hide. When I got home, I hauled my worn-out carcass, and my prize catch, to the garage and the first thing I did was weigh my striper.

What was left of it.

Its lower belly was blown out and its cavity was empty of most of its guts. The lower third of the bass was mostly gone, except for some tattered flaps of skin and meat, and protruding spine. Still, that ol' monster weighed-in at 69 pounds, 7 ounces. I took a picture of it, cleaned its cavity better, cleaned the beast and then threw it in the big freezer.

I contacted the world-record folks, but they weren't interested in anything but intact, weighable fish. My shot-up whopper was about 9-pounds shy of the world record, and my shot-up hide was about 9-pounds shy of any desire to ever go out there again and risk another run-in with that ol' rattlesnake-mean son-of-a-gun!

Trespassing isn't right, I know, but when you're young, and the fishing is THAT good … well, OK yeah, I did go back a few more times over the years. But I never encountered Old Rocksalt out there again; I later heard that he had died. I haven't been back there since, and now, looking back, I believe that in a crazy ol' way, Old Rocksalt had been part of the magic that the Secret Spot and the wetlands held for us local youngsters.

Speaking of local youngsters, I've heard that the buzz among the new crop of 'em, is that Old Rocksalt's "ghost" now haunts the wetlands at night. Ghost. Yeah, I know. But Dickey O'Shea and a few kids were out there night fishing awhile back, and got chased off by a crazy old man that they swear was Old Rocksalt. They said the shotgun blast was the first indication of his presence, and was what made fat Timmy Wilson dump a load right in his drawers. I'm not a real big believer in ghosts 'n all, but maybe I'll take a look out there some night when the moon is full and an exceptionally high tide is forecast … could be the makings for another notch on my belt of wild adventures, and another story that might be fun to tell my kids the first time I take 'em night fishing out on Old Rocksalt's land. Oh, it wouldn't be trespassing anymore, it's county property now, and open to the public. I don't know what the "ghost" of Old Rocksalt will have to say about all that. But we'll see …

Deus Absconditus

By: Brian Whitmer

Considering the conditions, we did better than I thought we would. We managed to get about 12,000 feet before one of us finally broke down and asked, "What the hell are we doing here?" And as much as I hate to admit it, I was the one who asked the question.

Neither Liz nor I had ever climbed a mountain before, but I had read somewhere that only about 20 percent of the people who attempt Mount Shasta are experienced mountaineers. Why spend all that money on lessons and equipment, I reasoned, when there are mountains such as this in glorious Northern California? With only a few treacherous snowfields and a couple of really steep pitches, Shasta was reputed to be a beginner's mountain—supposedly a "do-able" climb for anybody in decent physical condition. And that was us. We rented crampons and ice axes in the town named for the mountain, and we hit the road toward base camp.

The ranger who gave us our permit mentioned that weather is the biggest challenge on the mountain. It's the number one reason most climbing parties get turned back before reaching the summit. In fact, he added, half of those who try don't make it. He gestured toward the sky outside his window and suggested we keep a close eye on it. "It's been bad up there lately," he said. "Really unstable."

We didn't take his warning lightly, but Liz and I are experienced backpackers, so we were pretty confident in our hiking abilities and in our capacity to read the weather. For that reason, we were disappointed but not particularly worried when sleet iced over our base camp later that evening.

Horse Camp, as it is called, is near 7,000 feet, and it's hardly what we would consider remote. Our only concern that evening was that the weather might not clear up in time for us to get an early start to the summit in the morning, or, more likely, that the weather would be good enough for climbing, but not good enough for decent visibility at the top. On a good day, Shasta's 14,162-foot summit offers spectacular vistas and can be reached in about eight or nine hours. If the descent takes half that long, we figured, we'd need to start climbing well before dawn in order to be back at Horse Camp by nightfall. There was no question that we needed to be back by nightfall. We weren't taking anything but day packs beyond Horse Camp.

It was hard to get out of bed at 5 a.m. knowing that the world outside was glistening with ice—or would have been if there had been moonlight to reflect off of it. Extending an arm out of my warm sleeping bag, I pushed my finger into the tent wall until it touched the rainfly, and, as I expected, the fly was stiff until I applied enough pressure to crack the thin ice wafer that had formed on the other side. Despite the gloomy prospects for sightseeing, we got up anyway, packed, then started climbing. Without moon or stars for guidance or company, we began our nearly blind assault on the massive black presence of the mountain. There were many slick patches of ice on the rock, but we hoped for better conditions up above.

The first part of the climb was deceptively easy. It didn't take long, though, for things to start getting dicey. Neither of us had ever used crampons before, and we found them awkward and unwieldy. We also quickly tired of having to put them on and take them off repeatedly. They were rentals, though, so what the hell? We sometimes kept them on while crossing short stretches of bare rock and lava. Breathing was getting less and less satisfying with every gain in elevation, and the grade was getting steeper with every footfall. In addition, the wind was starting to gust up to speeds I couldn't even guess at, and it caused me to wonder if the expression "getting blown off the mountain" was more than just a mountaineering figure of speech. On top of all that, a headache was expanding rapidly behind my eyes, making it difficult to concentrate. I couldn't remember if this was a new development or if I'd had it when I woke up that morning. I didn't want to believe that I might be one of those people who is susceptible to mountain sickness.

To her credit, Liz kept plugging away at the slope, despite the fact that her heart was not totally into it. You see, whereas I was there to climb the mountain, Liz was there mostly to be with me. Mountain climbing wasn't her thing, but she was being a good sport because she knew I wanted to try it. It went that way with many of our shared activities. She preferred day hiking to backpacking, sea kayaking to white-water kayaking, downhill skiing to cross-country skiing. In other words, she enjoyed nature for its own sake, whereas I tended to use nature as a vehicle for physical challenge. Nevertheless, she always agreed to accompany me on my adventures, even the harebrained ones.

For this reason, it was quite a surprise when I found myself shouting at Liz to hold up, suggesting to her that we might want to abort the climb. We were at the base of Red Bank, an enormous rock outcropping a good 4,000 feet above timberline. The way up appeared almost vertical from there, and I didn't like the look of the clouds rolling over the top. I was also getting seriously concerned about the snowflakes that came whipping around the mountain at us like paint chips in a wind tunnel. They stung a little, and they made me wonder how much heavier the snow would have to get before we'd have trouble finding our way back down. It was time to reconsider.

I trudged over to Liz, but I still had to raise my voice to be heard over the wind. "I've got something for you," I said, fishing a slip of paper out of my anorak and smiling at my own foresightedness. "I thought we might need something more than PowerBars to get us over the top. Maybe these words of inspiration will do the trick."

Even through her sunglasses, I could see that her eyes were dancing and sparkling. Liz was a sucker for poetry and romance, and I fell short so often in that department that she got positively woozy whenever I thought to do something literary. Clinging tight to the paper, so the wind wouldn't snatch it away, I read: "In the mythic tradition, the mountain is the bond between Earth and Sky. Its solitary summit reaches the sphere of eternity, and its base spreads out in manifold foothills into the world of mortals. It is the way by which man can raise himself to the divine and by which the divine can reveal itself to man." I paused. "Rene Dumal."

She was delighted. About halfway through the reading, she leaned her forehead against mine and kept it there until after I'd finished. "I like that," she said, patting my chest with a mittened hand. "Thanks, Whit."

"Did it do the trick?" I asked.

"I don't know," she said, looking at the turbid sky. "God doesn't seem to want us storming heaven today. What do you think?"

It was a deceptively pointed question. It pretended to be about weather and climbing conditions, but it was partly about spiritual considerations. Liz and I had been together for almost two years by that time, and the reason we weren't married was due to our significant religious differences. We managed to gloss over them most of the time by avoiding the issue entirely or by keeping spiritual discussions nebulous and vague, nondenominational. But she was a Catholic and I was an atheist; how vague can you really be? Whenever I tried to meet her halfway on the spiritual plane, it confused her more than anything else. She didn't know if I was converting, compromising or being patronizing. Frankly, I wasn't sure myself. Readings such as the one I'd just produced from my pocket sometimes brought us closer together, sometimes they backfired. It was a bit of a crapshoot.

I stood for several minutes trying to size up the weather and the chute ahead of us, but I was distracted by my headache and frustrated by this ever-present obstacle to our relationship. I wasn't thinking clearly, and that, I concluded, was reason enough to turn back. "Let's return to the world of mortals," I said finally. "Besides, with this weather, we're not going to see anything from up there anyway."

Both wind and snowfall increased shortly after we began our descent; they seemed to be chasing us down the mountain, pushing us along, impatient for us to leave. The good news was that the wind evaporated some of the ice patches, and we were able to make better time over bare rock without crampons. We were practically hopping down the mountain when we encountered a long and steep snowfield called Climber's Gully. It looked like a narrow ski run, but it was still the best route down. We were moving so fast at the time that we didn't figure to be on it very long; therefore, we decided to try crossing it without stopping to put on our crampons. Instead, just as an added safety precaution, I threw a loop of rope around Liz and tied the other end to my waist. Like I said, we had no experience as mountaineers.

We stepped into Climber's Gully with heavy, forceful strides, stomping down with each heel to create a level stair step to stand on. It was a technique we had learned on a backpacking trip in the Montana Rockies. I went first, and Liz tried to step in my footprints. Before I went 10 steps, though, I realized we might have a problem. The snow was glazed with a layer of ice, and sometimes my foot nearly glanced off of it, trying to slip out from under me instead of biting into the snow underneath. I was also having trouble with visibility. I was losing the contrast between the snow on the ground and the snow in the wind. It was getting hard to see the angle of the slope below me, hard to know where to expect my foot to meet the ice.

"I don't like this," I hollered over my shoulder. "Let's put on the crampons." Then, like the novices we were, we both sat down on the slope. I realized even before I saw Liz slip that one of us should have clung tight to the snow while the other put on crampons, but it was too late to do it over again. That moment was gone. I guess when Liz sat down, that distributed her weight over the ice instead of anchoring her to one spot. She slid past me slowly but helplessly, her ice ax following her down just a few feet out of reach. "Falling!" she shouted with a touch of embarrassment in her voice. Then she began pounding at the ice with her mittens, and she let out an exasperated sound when she couldn't stop herself. Frantically, I started reeling in the rope. I stopped a second to grab my own ax, then went back to the rope again. But it was too late. In seconds, Liz was racing away at incredible speed, and when the slack came out of the rope, her momentum snapped me off the mountain like I was a water skier.

We were at the bottom of Climber's Gully in no time at all.

* * * * * *

I was trained as a First Responder years ago, when I first started spending a lot of time in wilderness settings. My certification had expired long before Liz and I went up Mount Shasta, but I was sure glad to have had the initial training when I shook off the stars at the bottom of Climber's Gully and started assessing our injuries. I could see right away that Liz had a broken shin. I thought I had come out unscathed, but while I was checking Liz for other injuries, she informed me that I had a lot of blood on my face. There was blood on my ice ax, too, but my face wound seemed to be a broad scrape, not a puncture. Either way, it wasn't serious, just ugly.

I didn't like the jagged look of the lump under the skin of her leg, so I decided to realign the bones before splinting the shin. Since that involves pulling gently on a very tender leg, I carefully explained what I was doing before jumping in. Fortunately, Liz trusted me and soon discovered that a little traction reduces the pain rather than increasing it. It was something of a happy surprise for me, too. I'd been taught all this in simulations, of course, but I had never actually done it before. The stress of the procedure got me sweating despite the cold. I can only guess at how it affected Liz. Still, it was a great relief to eventually behold a realigned and properly splinted leg, and to see that Liz was in fairly high spirits, to boot.

I found a protected nook in some boulders at the base of the gully and moved Liz there to get her out of the wind. We moved along surprisingly well considering her injury. She put her arm around my neck and leaned most of her weight on my shoulder. Once I got her comfortable and smiling, I went out to retrieve the gear. By the time I got back, though, her mood had definitely changed. "We're not going to make it back by nightfall," she said somewhat absently, unzipping her little day pack and fishing around in it. "And we don't have what we need to stay up here overnight." I noticed that she wasn't looking for anything in particular in the pack; she was just taking inventory. For the first time since our fall, it was sinking in that we were in pretty serious trouble. I started shuffling through my pack, too. There wasn't much in it.

We spent a good hour there, hunkered down in our nearly wind-proof nook, eating lunch and weighing our survival options. We thought we might make it through the night if we could get a fire going, and if we didn't get another sleet squall like the night before. On the other hand, the weather seemed to be getting worse, and there wasn't much to fuel a fire at an elevation of 9,000 feet. Also, I didn't like the idea of waiting until tomorrow, when we would be hungrier and weaker, to make the treacherous descent. It was doubt-ful either one of us would get any sleep, and who knows how much of Liz's energy would be sapped by the pain of the broken leg. Another nagging worry was the possibility of internal bleeding. I couldn't see any evidence of it, but how could I know for sure? The benefits of waiting didn't seem worth the risks.

"If the weather doesn't break by dawn tomorrow," I said, thinking out loud, "then we won't have bought anything by staying the night. We'll have more daylight to work with, I suppose, but visibility stinks with or without it."

Liz pondered that for a while. "So we leave now, and finish the last part of the descent in the dark?"

"I don't like your wording," I said, squirming a little, "but yeah, that's the way I see it."

"Then we better get going, I guess," she said, being a trooper.

Our trek down the mountain was tedious and laborious. Our pace was unbearably slow, movement impossibly difficult, and night fell long before I expected it to. We experimented with a variety of carry and assist techniques, some classic and some innovative, but all of which failed to produce lasting progress. We stopped frequently for short rests and water breaks, and it got harder and harder to stand up again after each one. We stopped for a somewhat longer break just as the sun was setting to power up on gorp and candy bars. It was all we had left. Snow was falling in earnest by then, and we had to shake it off every few minutes to keep it from building up on us. We were both sweaty, and the wind gave us chills, so we sat on the leeward side of a large boulder. I wasn't sure exactly where we were. Our situation could have been worse, I suppose, but that was no consolation. We were in deep shit.

"Your beard's caked with blood," said Liz, reaching out for my face, but not quite touching it.

"It's nothing," I replied casually, wondering, though, if I'd be so cavalier without the numbing cold to mask the pain. "How's the leg?"

"Weird," she said, poking at the splint. "It feels kind of numb, but it hurts like hell, too."

"You want me to loosen it again?"

"No, I think it's all right." She slumped her head against my shoulder, sending a cascade of snow to my lap. "The good leg hurts more than the broken one," she said, massaging it. "It's really sore, and I don't know if I can go any farther."

I was exhausted, too. I wasn't sure if I could stand up again. My thighs burned from exertion, and my knees ached from the pound of the descent. I unwrapped a small, unsatisfying candy bar and fought the urge to say something fatalistic, like, "What was on the menu at the Last Supper anyway?" Or, "Liz, can you ever forgive me for bringing you up here?" She deserved an apology, of course, but I thought that to give her one now would be a negative thought—an admission that we were done for—and we couldn't afford to think along those lines. It was Liz who finally broke the ice. "We're going to need a miracle," she said softly.

I wasn't thinking in religious terms at that point, but it seemed she was. "I don't think ..." She stopped, suddenly near tears, and tried again. "I don't ... think we're going to get a miracle, though."

There was a long pause I couldn't fill. Then she added weakly, "I don't think God's up here on the mountain."

I was stunned, but didn't show it. Those had to have been the hardest words she ever uttered. I pretended to brush back some of her hair from her face just as an excuse to touch her. "No," I said, almost whispering, "I guess he's not here." We sat listening to the wind for a while, and then I added something else. "Not today."

We held each other as the enormous black shadow of the mountain swallowed the last light of day.

* * * * *

Martin Luther coined the Latin expression *"deus absconditus"* to refer to the hidden nature of God, and I reflect from time to time that one's faith is rather dependent upon how one responds to that hidden nature. To some, like Martin Luther and Liz, I suppose, it means that God's presence is imperceptible and unknowable. To others, like me, it means that he's not even there—that he's just the product of wishful thinking. Deus absconditus. God absconded. I like the expression. It certainly suited our tenuous situation up on that mountain. It's what made Liz doubt her beliefs, and it's what made me wish I was wrong about mine. In that sense, it brought us a lot closer together.

After a while, I shook the snow off my hood and leaned down to kiss Liz on the forehead. Then I looked her in the face with raised eyebrows as if it say, "Time to go?"

She gazed up into my eyes with an expression that was the very definition of submission. "Get me out of here, Whit."

* * * * *

It's funny how long two people who know each other well can perpetuate a complete misunderstanding. All the rest of the way down the mountain, I thought about what Liz had said to me, and I concluded that she had lost a significant portion of her faith that night. I believe that when she asked me to save her and resigned herself to the probability that no miracles were coming our way, she was in a sense renouncing God who had apparently abandoned her. I never asked her about this directly because I didn't want her to feel I was rubbing her nose in it, saying, "I told you so." And because of my hesitation, the myth persisted for several months. It was a simple nickname, of all things, that finally got us talking about what that day on the mountain really meant to each of us. But I'll get to that.

Looking back, I think I finally got us to safety by luck and by deciding to forget about trying to get back to Horse Camp. For all intents and purposes, we were lost the moment we fell down Climber's Gully. The likelihood of finding our little campsite after that was remote. On the other hand, I figured we stood a pretty good chance of finding the trail that connected Horse Camp to the road down the mountain, or maybe even the road itself. These were much bigger targets, and the way down would be obvious once we found either one of them. And that's just what we did. Several other climbers were sorting their gear at the trailhead when we staggered out of the woods late the next morning. Two of them drove us to town.

When we finally ended our grueling descent and arrived at the emergency room, we were barely recognizable as human beings. Still, Liz smiled at me through the fog of pain as the doctor cut apart her bandages and separated her swollen leg from the splint. She grabbed my collar and pulled my frost-nipped, windburned face down to hers. "You did good, Eskimo," she whispered. "I love you, Eskimo." She's called me that ever since.

For months, I didn't give the name much thought. I just assumed that it referred to the frigid conditions we'd managed to survive. For that reason, I started calling her Blizzard. Nearly half a year after the incident, though, I finally asked Liz why she was so stuck on calling me Eskimo. I got a startling answer.

"Thought you'd never ask," she said, pushing me into a chair and perching herself on the footstool in front of me. "It's from a story I heard a long time ago—kind of a joke, I suppose. It goes like this: "A guy is complaining to his minister that God has forsaken him, and he's mad as hell about it. 'What makes you say that?' asks the minister.

" 'Well, I was on a mountain in Alaska last month with no food or water,' says the guy, 'and I got lost in a blizzard.'

" 'Yes, go on,' says the minister.

" 'Anyway, I figured I was a goner, so I prayed to God for help. I told him that if he rescued me with a miracle, I'd be his most faithful servant for the rest of my life.' The guy slams his fist down, really angry.

"The minister's confused. 'But what makes you say God has forsaken you? Here you are, in perfect health. Surely God worked a miracle and saved you.'

"The guy scoffs at the minister. 'A miracle!' he shouts. 'I didn't get any damned miracle. God left me to die!'

" 'Well, what happened?' asks the minister.

" 'Aw,' says the guy, 'some damned Eskimo finally came along and rescued me.' "

Liz sat smiling, waiting for a response, as I processed the import of what she'd just told me. At first I was almost horrified, wondering if she had misunderstood me as much as I misunderstood her. What did she think I meant, I wondered, when I responded to her statement about God not being on the mountain by saying, "Not today?" Did she think I was converting, compromising or being patronizing? I wasn't even sure myself. Unbelievably, we seemed to be right back where we started on the religion issue.

But then I had a thought—something of a revelation, if you will. I opened my arms, and Liz slipped between them and into my lap. I stroked her hair and wondered if it really made any difference at all. God has absconded. No one lives in Eden anymore. It's up to each of us to decide for ourselves if we are tools in the hands of a higher power. Personally, I still don't believe it. But so what if Liz does? Does it diminish me to be seen that way? I don't think so. In fact, it might do just the opposite. After all, it's not every day that you get a chance to be somebody's guardian angel. It's not every day you get to say you've come down from the mountaintop on a mission from God.

Eco-Challenge An Exercise in Perceived Mortality

By: Michael Hodgson

Jay Smith's eyes steeled under the harsh low-angle glare of a late afternoon Utah sun. His right foot scuffed and stirred the sand in front of him as I waited expectantly for his assessment of our day of training.

"Well, Michael, the good news is that four of you lived."

I waited for the inevitable bad news that was destined to follow.

Jay ran his hands through wind-tousled hair. "Unfortunately, one of you died—twice."

Not exactly an auspicious beginning, nor the confidence builder I had hoped for. There were only two weeks to go until the start of the Eco-Challenge, and our team of five journalists was beginning to look more like sacrificial lambs than ardent competitors in search of a grand story.

My sphincter tightened appreciably at the thought of having to watch out for a decidedly inexperienced team member while working my own way up a 1,200-foot lifeline using Jumars and etries. One mistake could certainly put a damper on any future plans for life—and I had been having such a good day.

I had first heard of the Eco-Challenge in early 1994, when the course promoter, Mark Burnett, asked me if I was interested in covering the event for the magazines I write for, *Outdoor Retailer* and *Adventure West*. The event intrigued me. Teams of five, with at least one woman or man on every team, would travel non-stop together over 370 miles of rugged wild Utah lands, navigating by map and compass, and passing through various passport control points in sequence. They would cross this terrain by mountaineering rope, canoe, white-water raft, mountain bike, foot and horse (three horses for five teammates, so two are always on foot). The route would take teams into remote canyons where swimming through bitter cold water while dragging your pack is the only path, up and down steep rock walls more than 1,000 feet high, through intense rapids, and over hot and arid sand flats. Never one for the sidelines when a real game beckons, I brazenly informed Mark that I would love to cover the event, but only as a participant. So it was that I became the founding and sole member of Team Media, and since there were no other members to dispute or challenge the claim, I received the billing as the team captain to boot—a captain of a team of one.

Not until March 13, 1995—only seven weeks before the April 25 start of the race—did the team meet and become an official entity. Team Media, race number 84, consisted of: Johnny Dodd, *People Magazine*; Dan Glick, *Newsweek* and *Eco Traveler*; Roy Wallack, *Triathlete Magazine* and *Men's Journal*; and Beth Howard, a freelancer who would be writing a story for *Self*. Although all of us had a relatively strong outdoor adventure background, none of us were hardened athletes and none of us had been training for what some would bill as "a race from hell." We had never spent any time together as a team, were decidedly inexperienced in a number of the venus we would have to complete to survive, and there was no way we would be able to train properly to gain even the most basic level of experience that savvy race participants would deem vital to success.

What we lacked in experience, though, we made up for in unbridled enthusiasm—we were obviously deranged and quite in need of professional help, and we were no doubt too stupid to realize that we had no chance for success. But then, that is what professional outdoor adventure journalists' lives are built around—pure, unadulterated blind faith and the devout belief that anything is possible as long as a good story hangs in the balance. Worry? Nahhh! A little death never hurt anyone, hah, hah.

Thus began my personal 10-day immersion course in perceived mortality. Lesson One began on the rocks in Utah, as I watched my eager, yet dangerously inexperienced teammate defy logic and continue to lunge and grunt dangerously up and down the fixed ropes. He seemed unfazed by the fact that he had just "died twice" and continued to assert that with a little more time he could master ascending and descending and the required knot transfers that would be necessary on the 1,200-foot route we anticipated during the race. I had no doubt that he could learn the skills, but not in two weeks and not so well that I could trust he would be able to remember critical sequences while clinging to a rock wall 500 feet off the deck with only six hours of sleep in a 48-hour time frame that would be jammed full of adrenaline-pumping action and physical stress. Death only comes once and you don't get a replay.

Although the race organizers offered to let the four of us climb while trucking the other teammate around the climbing zones, we declined. This event was as much about teamwork as it was about physical effort, and there was no way we would allow anyone to split the team, for any reason.

Thirty minutes before the race, with a helmet perched jauntily on my head and a weighted pack sagging on my back, I began Lesson Two. My tutor was a horse that had no intention of remaining calm as long as his 149 other brethren were snorting, whinnying and doing their level best to toss any rider who attempted to sit tall in the saddle. I am convinced that the only reason these horses from

Montana were so upset is that no self-respecting range horse that had herded cattle all over the West and had lived a wild and hardy life would take pride in being mounted by urban cowboys wearing stupid white helmets and dressed in Lycra tights and technicolor jerseys. One look at the Good Morning America and MTV camera crews hovering around like vultures and these horses decided to execute an organized revolt—give us real cowboys or give us hay!

Eco-Challengers were spending just as much time performing unplanned and spectacular dismounts as they were sitting astride leather saddles with clenched cheeks. As if to bold-stamp his displeasure with the entire morning experience, Caramel, my steed for the next 28 miles decided to experiment by attempting to launch a human sans spacecraft into orbit right in front of the TV cameras. Fortunately, I anticipated his move and managed to execute a remarkable butt-to-stomach-with-a-half-twist-knee-to-mouth dismount that, bless their little souls, the camera crew wanted me to replicate since they weren't sure they had captured the essence of the first time round. Of course, ordinarily I would have been happy to oblige, but since it felt as if a few teeth were now missing and I thought they might be essential parts of my body over the next few days, I elected to find my teeth first, locate the publicity second. As it turned out, my teeth had remained intact. It was my brain that had become detached.

I didn't need any convincing to remain dismounted from my horse and lead him for the first three miles of the race. If I couldn't knock any sense into him, I could sure as heck try to walk the jumpiness out. As we walked along, with Beth riding since her equestrian experience had earned her mount's respect, I began to feel as though I were trekking along a road in the Civil War, lined with wretched remnants of a defeated regiment. Everywhere I looked, loose horses rambled, sometimes with a defiant rider in hot pursuit. Beaten Eco-Challengers limped onward, their gazes fixed 20 miles or so down the road to the next checkpoint, the next tangible goal. Those who remained astride their steeds, butts slapping saddle leather in an awkward rhythm that sometimes matched their horse's gait, sometimes not, uniformly adopted the Eco-Challenge equestrian mantra: "OW, OW, OW, whoa, whoa, whoa, OW, OW, OW, whoa ... I said

Whoa ... slow down damnit ... OW, OW, OW ... oh God, can I run now ... please?!" It was a mantra that I became all too familiar with once I found my place in the saddle. Not since having my backside paddled by Mr. Bump, my sixth grade teacher, and his infamous wooden swatter had I felt such an ache. Thank God, my teammates allowed me to run much of the way! Goodbye horses. Hello death march and canyoneering.

As terra firma vanished from under foot and icy cold water, 47 degrees to be exact, closed over my head, I realized that Lesson Three was about to begin. While there are definite moments when it is an advantage to being 5 foot, 6 inches tall, this was not one of those times. Another 6 inches or so and I would be able to walk with my nose pushed above the water's surface like a periscope, sucking in life-giving air. As it was, I was in desperate need of gills unless I could find a way to float, and soon. Kicking and spluttering I clambered aboard my pack which floated awkwardly in the turgid, brown water of the San Rafael. As a child, I had enjoyed watching the desperate antics of ants, spiders and other various forms of insects clinging desperately to a bobbing twig or leaf which I had tossed irreverently into the many streams that ribboned the summer camp I attended. Mother Nature now appeared to be exacting a karmic revenge—note to my daughter ... be kind to all living creatures you encounter.

Not thrilled with the prospect of ending my days trapped in a slick-walled watery prison, I kicked like there was no tomorrow toward the far end of this deep canyon section where solid footing and only waist-deep water beckoned. Stumbling, spluttering and cursing, I arose from the depths with water dripping from every part of my body including a few places I had no idea water could drip from. I looked, I am sure, like some nightmarish creature rising from the watery depths of a B-grade, late-night horror movie. As I attempted to swing my pack to my shoulders, I made an interesting discovery. Either I had become incredibly weakened by my efforts to swim through water even a polar bear would shy away from or my pack had somehow acquired roots. No matter how hard I lifted, the pack just sat there. As I pondered this latest development, the pack began grinning at me—really. It just sat there, grinning a Cheshire cat grin. Fatigue and hunger had nothing to do with this apparition, I am sure. Tired and by now getting quite pissed off, I gave the shoulder straps of my pack-cum-Cheshire-cat a final heave and it lifted off the ground, water pouring from every seam and small zipper openings. Oh goody! Now I get to carry a pack full of river water. I could only hope that my warm clothes and sleeping bag (something I would critically need hours later as I staved off the initial encroachments of hypothermia) remained dry.

This had become more than just a race. We were each trekking across a landscape of extremes on an almost numbing excursion through the depths and catacombs of a mind trying to cope with thirst, hunger, pain, fatigue and frustration. We began existing for simple victories. Small things brought smiles: Finding water; eating a PowerBar; nurturing a discarded apple discovered on the trail; arriving successfully at a Passport Control Point to the accompanying cheers of other teams; discovering during a potty break that you could actually squat and deliver solid waste and not the squirty liquid shit that had been with you every hour on the hour since drinking river water 36 hours earlier.

Sixty or so odd miles and approximately 40 hours later, the canyons and cold river were but a faint memory. Our water gone, dry tongues licked cracked lips in anticipation of an upcoming spring where we could replenish our supplies and quench our thirst. We rounded the bend and gazed upon the oasis—an oil-slicked, mosquito-infested sludge pond containing a few odd tires, tons of cattle excrement, and one dead and bloated rat ... yummy. Lesson Four was about to begin. Other teams were scattered about, staring glumly at what could only loosely, very loosely, be defined as a spring. I'd seen waste collection ponds in city treatment plants that appeared infinitely more drinkable than this container of scum. Unfortunately, necessity is born of misery and we needed water. Out came the filters and slowly, excruciatingly slow, we pumped water, one quart at a time, adding iodine as a safety and cleaning the filter every quart because it had clogged with the silt and sludge. We managed to filter two gallons in just over an hour when an Eco-

Challenge vehicle arrived and announced that they would be providing water to drink at the next Passport Control Point, three miles distant—terrific timing, guys!

This had become a war of attrition. Dehydration, hypothermia, blown-out knees, broken bones and more had claimed members from nearly 15 teams up to this point. We arrived at Passport Control 8 feeling surprisingly chipper. While we drank our fill of pure water, I couldn't help but notice many of the eyes of other teams. Some were determined, focused on the goal, shifting confidently from map to pack to watch. Others were blank, as if all feeling and emotion had been erased from the mental slate. A few looked as though they belonged to a deer, caught in the headlights of an oncoming car. There would be many more to fall before the night was through.

Blazo Blues

By: Mary Bedingfieldsmith

This whole adventure began as a result of being too young to know any better. You see, we're from Utah. That's the state where we had a beautiful place called Glen Canyon. Now "they" tell us we have a beautiful place called Lake Powell and the twisting, enticing cathedral-like canyon that it used to be is now a magnificent sewage lagoon disguised as a motorboat paradise. A book of photographs by Elliot Porter showed us the treasure, now-submerged, that no one really knew and that is no more. Back in the '60s, I guess its anonymity made it an easy sacrificial lamb in exchange for the then also threatened Dinosaur National Park and Grand Canyon. So it was gone before we ever knew it.

But in the early '80s, when Scott and I learned of the Reagan Administration's scheme to dredge up the coastal plain of Alaska's Arctic National Wildlife Refuge (ANWR) for a few buckets of oil, we vowed to see that wild place and spread the word so bulldozers and oil drills couldn't claim another irreplaceable gem.

We worked insane schedules to save up the money we needed to leave our jobs, drive to Fairbanks and hire a bush pilot to fly us to ANWR.

So here we were, many miles north of the Arctic Circle. "One ... two ... three ... four ... five ... six," I counted as we heaved the last of our gear bags from the conveyor belt at Prudhoe Bay's airport.

It seemed this chant had become a ritualistic incantation since we had packed for the flight from Fairbanks several days earlier. Living in the back of our pickup en route to Alaska had required a lot of gear juggling—and, as we found out, many opportunities to lose things to the God of Disorganization along the way. We had to make certain all "the gear" arrived with us, since we were about to spend three weeks in BIG wilderness—no hiking out to a trailhead if we forgot something essential.

We had gone over our lists several times and arranged the gear into six pieces of luggage. We counted it every time we moved it—packing the truck, unloading, checking onto the plane, unloading again. Hence the mantra ... one (ammo can with Scott's cameras, and later to be our bear-resistant, odor-proof food container), two (ammo can of film), three (tent), four (duffel bag of food), five (my backpack of clothing and Arctic miscellany), six (Scott's backpack of assorted necessaries).

Now, after all those months of planning, after all those miles of sitting in the cab of a four-cylinder pickup, we were almost there. Alaska's Arctic National Wildlife Refuge was only a few more countdowns away.

A year and a half earlier, we had contacted a bush pilot we had read about in some "How To Do It Right" outdoor magazine. We had spoken on several occasions, each time armed with a long list of questions: Where's the best drop point? How much is the fare? How long is the flight? How many mosquitoes can we expect? Can we carry fuel on the plane? If not, can we get it from you? He always gave satisfactory answers.

However, since we wanted arrangements finalized before we drove for weeks and thousands of miles, each conversation ended with Scott asking, "When do you want a deposit for the flight?"

The reply never changed: "Don't worry about it. We'll take care of you when you get here."

I thought, "What a nice man."

On August 1, when we arrived in Fairbanks, our golden moment, the day we were to be dropped off on the tundra, was only three days away. We drove directly to the airport and walked the length of the terminal looking for our contact. After three passes, we noticed an unlit counter emblazoned with the name of the company. A small handwritten message taped next to a dusty phone told us to dial the indicated number for information.

We hurriedly dialed and listened, but received only unanswered ringing in return. Looks of confusion passed between Scott and me. "Try again," I suggested optimistically. "Maybe we made a mistake."

Scott called again. More ringing. Now a little cursing from us.

Finally a woman at the next desk, probably reacting to the loud crash of the receiver in the cradle and then even louder expletives, explained that our bush pilot had left the area with the planes and assets of his business, the unpaid-for gas of another company, and the deposit money of several now-dissatisfied customers. She hoped we weren't any of those.

At first, we sighed with relief because we had never paid a deposit and explained our situation. Then, with a sigh of despair, we asked if she could help with our dilemma. We were to have flown from Fairbanks directly to Kaktovik, a small native village on the Barter Island, and from there to the coastal plain. Now how were we to get to ANWR? She smiled and handed us a phone number.

Marty MacDonald listened knowingly. (He'd probably heard the same story from a number of other stranded unfortunates.) Martin Air, his company, could fly us from Prudhoe Bay to Kaktovik in a small plane and then into the refuge on an even smaller craft. He explained we couldn't drive the last corridor from Fairbanks to Prudhoe Bay because it was closed to public travel unless we could obtain, in three days, a rare permit. "Buy two commercial tickets on Alaska Air. You can't bring white gas on its plane, but we'll get you some when you get here." He gave us short list of things, finished by quoting the price, then hung up.

"But that's twice as much money ...," Scott started to say. By then, though, no one was listening.

At dinner that night in a state park in the center of Fairbanks, illuminated by the comforting glow of our Coleman lantern, we decided that, even if we had to work at Bob's Burger Bar to earn enough money to get home, we'd be on that plane.

One ... two ... three ... four ... five ... six. Scott hauled the gear from Prudhoe Bay's waiting room and I loaded it into the back of Martin Air's courtesy taxi, a mud-spattered pickup. Only two more flights to go.

I suppose Marty MacDonald had heard a bit more of that rushed phone conversation than we had thought. Or maybe he recognized a shoestring adventure as he watched us lug makeshift "How To Do It Right" gear containers through the blowing sleet into his hangar. Or perhaps he had once worked at Bob's Burger Bar himself.

Whatever the reason, the next morning as we clambered into his six-seater Cessna, Marty explained that, free of charge, the state of Alaska was flying us to Kaktovik, only 30 miles from our goal.

It seemed the governor was also flying to the island that day. His agenda: to convince the natives that Chevron and Exxon really cared about them as long as they had oil in their backyard. And, a lot of money could make the upheaval of their culture temporarily painless.

All that aside, there were empty seats on the governor's chartered plane—a tight but cozy squeeze for the two of us and our luggage behind the government officials. Marty helped us load our six containers. We made sure he also loaded the requested Blazo, our white gas in its distinctive blue can. With a wave, Marty headed back to the hangar to his paying customers while Steve, Martin Air's second pilot, taxied us down the runway.

At Kaktovik, with the waters of the Arctic Ocean lapping at our boots and six pieces of assorted luggage and one blue can nearby, we looked inland and discussed the dense fog bank that obscured everything to the south. I thought we'd have to wait for better weather. However, Steve said he could still fly but he wasn't overly optimistic about the forecast.

The final leg of our trip had to be taken one passenger at a time in a Piper Super Cub, a tiny plane that was little more than a metal frame wrapped in cloth. Total capacity: one pilot, one passenger and part of our gear. Steve would take Scott at an altitude of 38 feet, just below the 40-foot ceiling. The only problem was, if the weather went to hell, Scott would be alone on the tundra while I was stuck in the village waiting.

While Steve readied the Super Cub, Scott and I rummaged through everything making sure he had the required gear for him to solo for a day or two if necessary. Fifteen minutes later, Steve, Scott and three of the six pieces of luggage disappeared into the whiteness. I searched the skies, took a deep breath and headed for Martin Air's warming shack.

An hour later, the fog had lifted. The forecast had improved. The flying would be perfect. One ... two ... three ... pieces of luggage, and the blue can of Blazo barely fit stuffed under and behind me. Wiping my breath from the side window, I watched the coastal plain pass under me mile by mile—the last miles. We were both almost there.

Circling above the "landing strip," the smoothest 200 feet of tundra in the neighborhood, I saw Scott waving below. Obviously there had been no immediate need to set up camp, since he'd left his gear on the runway, still packed, and scouted the area for water and the perfect location for our base camp. His camera clicked madly to document every detail of our first "real day" on the ADVENTURE.

The plane bumped to a stop. I handed out a backpack, a duffel bag and the last ammo can. Steve, anxious to get hunters whose pickup had been delayed for five days due to snow, asked if we had everything. The familiar count. "One ... two ... three ... four ... five ... six. Yep. We're all set. See you in three weeks."

The plane's roar dwindled and disappeared. We were left with the grand solitude we'd come so far to find. Emerald green surrounded us on all sides. Itkilyariak Creek led inland to the Sadlerochit Mountains and Mount Chamberlin, the second highest peak in the Brooks Range. Tombstone Valley lay hidden to the west. No noise, no people, no schedules, no clocks, and ... NO FUEL! The newly acquired number seven, Blazo stove fuel, had flown away with Steve, safely and securely stashed way back in the tail section. Now we were facing three weeks of raw noodles and not-so-hot chocolate.

Always the calming influence in all my emotional storms, Scott began setting up camp, transferring cameras and film to the tent, placing food into the ammo cans, and packing them far downwind of our chosen kitchen site, a nook in the 50-foot-high embankment at the edge of the creek's floodplain.

Tidy even when panicked, I rolled out the Therm-a-Rests, laid out the sleeping bags, and set out the books, journals, clothing and bulging stuff sacks we'd brought over such a distance. I heard Scott approach the tent whistling. Whistling!

"Hand me that red stuff sack. Here's part of our solution." And he extracted a full, liter fuel bottle from the bag. "There," he said, pointing to the dwarf willows in the dry creek bed, "is the rest of our answer."

"How'd you get that fuel? We CAN'T burn the willows!"

"I put it in my pack in Fairbanks just in case there wasn't much available at Prudhoe Bay. We'll conserve it and burn as few willows as possible. We don't have any other choice."

Over a tiny twig fire that first evening, we prepared a quick-cook, noodle dinner and gazed out across the coastal plain toward Camden Bay. I really wished about half a bucket of that oil the industrialists promised was there would magically materialize by morning.

The next morning, after cold oatmeal and tepid hot chocolate (conserving fuel), our wanderings took us to Tombstone Valley, an eerily eroded ancient landslide with standing monoliths reminiscent of headstones. We lingered at each monument searching for birds, collecting flowers and taking photos. The can of Blazo was long forgotten.

As we returned to camp after our daylong excursion, Scott led the way back while I stopped every few feet to collect cloud berries for dessert. A yell hurried me along and I saw Scott standing at the edge of the embankment above our tent. I made out his words as he pointed: "Hey, look at that. Is that what I think it is?"

I strained to see the mysterious IT, at last spotting a bluish something a couple hundred yards away. Jokingly, I said: "Yeah, I see it. Arctic litter in Blazo blue. Very funny. Now we've got Blazo popping up all over."

Laughing, we turned away and admired the reddening sky as we made our way down the steep slope to our tent. By now, we each had a large handful of pale yellow berries which we savored one by one. We dropped our packs and changed our soggy boots for dry shoes. A few minutes later, popping the last Arctic treats into our mouths, we strolled over to investigate. As we approached we saw it was, indeed, a Blazo can, a smashed but leaking Blazo can containing only a few teaspoons of fuel. After some speculation as to how it got there, we decided Steve must have dropped it from the plane window. Why he had not landed was a mystery. We gingerly moved the can and poured what remained into our stove. "Nice try, Steve," we thought, but now we were sure this was all the fuel there was.

In the Arctic, in August, the sun DOES go down, but not far enough below the horizon for it to get truly dark. There was plenty of time and light for one more scramble up the embankment before another undercooked dinner. Thirty miles to the north, on the ocean we could see pack ice—a signal that winter was just a few weeks away, but springlike pink asters and blue butterflies clustered at our feet. This truly was a surprising place of contrast.

Turning to the south, we saw the last alpenglow leave Mount Chamberlin as the sun dipped below the Arctic Ocean for an hour or two. Suddenly Scott grabbed my arm, spun me around, pointed and exclaimed, "Another can of Blazo!"

Steve must have dropped a second can, this one into a small patch of cushioning willows. Rushing over, we saw that's exactly what it was, a dented and dirty, lovely blue, completely intact, more than halfway full can of that precious fluid … fuel. We sauntered back to camp swinging the can between us anticipating a fully cooked dinner prepared the "How To Do It Right" way.

Our three weeks passed far too quickly. It snowed on August 8, killing nearly every one of the notorious coastal plain mosquitoes. That touch of winter sent the tundra on its incredible transition from its summer greens to its autumn reds. We walked as far as we could every day—13 to 18 miles—in every possible direction, all the while recording the Arctic's magnificence in photos and words.

When Steve picked us up, we were pleased to see he was in a larger plane which meant he could get both of us and our gear out in one trip. As we flew, he explained that he had indeed discovered our fuel can crammed back in the tail while loading hunters' equipment that first day. The next day, filled to capacity, he flew over our camp. We weren't there waving rescue flags at him, so he guessed we weren't too worried. However, he couldn't land and deliver fuel because the runway was too short to take off with the weight he had on board. Cleverly, he split the white gas between two Blazo cans, passed low over camp, opened a window and dropped one can. He saw it hit hard, cartwheel and spray the tundra with its contents.

One more can. One more chance, One more pass. One more bombs away. This time success. He had hoped we'd found it.

Below we saw a circle of musk oxen, the bulls in this season in rut. Steve banked sharply, wing tip pointed to the center of the herd. Two bulls twisted and bucked, then charged each other and collided with a smash of horn we could nearly hear in the plane. They faced off again, the breeze ruffling their ground-length guard hairs.

I watched for a long time as the plane flew on. We'd seen a place that few people know, and it wasn't anonymous to us anymore. Listening to the drone of our small plane, I couldn't help but feel a twinge of guilt that I'd wished for that one gallon of fuel. Seeing the vast grandeur pass away beneath me, I suddenly realized that, even if it meant eating cold breakfasts and raw dinners or never flying again, leaving this place the way it was—big, wild, empty—would be a small price to pay.

Voyage to the Bottom of the Klamath

By: Bill Cross

Polly was levitating before my very eyes, rising steadily until she was perhaps 8 feet above me. This can't be happening, I thought. The gods wouldn't do this to me. For an instant, she looked down at me with a puzzled expression, a question on her lips. Then the vision abruptly disappeared, replaced by a swirl of bubbles and then darkness as the raft overturned and all hell generally broke loose.

Actually, it had started breaking loose the day before, when we embarked on what was supposed to be a routine commercial raft trip down the Klamath River in Northern California. I had spent the better part of my summer on the Kern River, guiding customers down demanding Class IV and Class V white water. The stress of shepherding people through big, dangerous rapids had gradually taken its toll. I was starting to approach each new trip like a World War II bomber pilot heading out on another mission over Germany. Except I was dodging boulders, not flak. I was burned out, and I

desperately needed some R&R. So I signed up to lead a trip on the Lower Klamath—three days on a relaxing, mellow Class III. And I invited my sweetie, Polly, to join me.

The gods let us get precisely four miles down the Klamath before they decided it was time to have a little fun with the mortals. I had just taken my paddle raft through Devil's Toenail and I turned to watch the other boats come through. My sister, Diane, also a guide, was bringing up the rear in one of the big oar boats that hauled all the food and overnight gear. She pulled to shore above the rapid and jogged up the bank to get a better look at the drop. Suddenly, she started waving wildly, then dashed back to the boat and rowed through the rapid. When she pulled into the eddy below, it was obvious something was wrong: she was beet red, sweaty, wheezing and—there's no way to put this delicately—she had suddenly lost her figure. In fact, to put it bluntly, she was swelling up like a blowfish.

As Diane gasped out her story, we realized with horror that we had just witnessed "The Attack Of The Killer Hornets." It was not a pretty sight. I was reminded of the movie, *The Elephant Man*. We sat Diane down in the river to cool her off, but she just kept on bloating. Any minute, it seemed, she would lift off like a hot air balloon and drift out of the canyon. She was also having trouble breathing, as anaphylactic shock set in. We needed to do something fast. One of the passengers, a nurse, asked whether anyone had any drugs that might help slow the allergic reaction. The response was remarkable. The other passengers rummaged through their ditty bags and came up with baggies full of white powder and green herbs, Valium, little yellow pills ... no wonder they were having such a hard time learning right and left turns in the paddle boat! One woman fumbled frantically through her bag, then triumphantly held up a little tube and asked whether vaginal itching cream would help.

Sensing that these were not the cures for what ailed her, we decided to evacuate Diane. Polly and I flagged down a car and got her to the nearest settlement, where a backwoods doctor reversed the reaction with epinephrine injections. When we finally got back to the river, it was late afternoon, and we needed to hustle to make camp before dark. But after all the epinephrine, Diane was like a drunk in detox: woozy, disoriented and in no condition to row. So we propped her up in the front of the big baggage raft where, from her vantage point wedged between watertight bags, she mumbled directions to Polly, who had never rowed a boat in her life. At each rapid, Diane would rouse herself to moan and mutter like Ahab shouting deliriously about the white whale: "There! Look! Do you see it? More on the right oar, the right oar ... Oh God!"

That was Day One.

The next morning, I awoke with renewed hope for my relaxing little vacation on the Klamath. Lightning wouldn't strike twice, I told myself, not on this easy run. Unfortunately, the gods were just getting warmed up.

In order to get some quality time alone with my sweetheart, I decided to row lead in the baggage raft. And because this was the Mellow Klamath—not the Killer Kern—I was fairly casual about tying in my load. When someone brought the frying pan and Dutch oven over to my boat at the last minute (they had been overlooked in the rush to break camp), I didn't bother to untie the kitchen box and lock them inside. Instead, I simply wedged them into a couple of convenient gaps between watertight bags—the equivalent of a kid shoving his dirty laundry under the bed. I did the same with my sweater, and even with the guitar bag that another guide, Alan, brought up at the last moment. Thank goodness this is the Klamath, I thought smugly, so I don't have to retie the whole damn load.

At last the final items were stuffed into place, the petty annoyances of my job were behind me, and I looked forward to a day alone with my dear one. Polly sat atop the mountain of gear in the bow and we made eyes at each other. She was perched pretty high up there—guess I hadn't packed the load very efficiently—but no matter. Today would be an easy one: no rapids of note except Dragon's Tooth, and that was still well downstream.

There I was, drifting along all dreamy and content, when the gods started playing games again. I started thinking about the campsite at Ukonom Creek. If I was really going to impress Polly, I should definitely show her the falls at Ukonom. To miss that would be like skipping the Eiffel Tower on a tour of Paris. But you couldn't really make that side hike unless you camped at the mouth of the creek, and the site was only big enough for one group. We were just ahead of another commercial trip, and I suspected they might have the same destination in mind. How could I be sure of getting to Ukonom before them?

When we stopped for lunch, my heart sank as I watched the other group float past. Surely now they would go straight down and stake out Ukonom. But after lunch, my spirits rebounded when we passed the other group having their lunch! This was our big chance! There was only one problem: just downstream was Dragon's Tooth, the biggest rapid on the run. Standard procedure would be to stop and scout it, especially since I had only seen it a couple of times before, at much higher flows. But what if the other group decided to run it without scouting? Then they would leapfrog ahead and get that camp—*my* camp! I desperately wanted to take Polly on a personal tour of Ukonom Creek, and in my memory, Dragon's Tooth was an easy right-side run. So I cruised past the scouting eddy.

As we rounded the bend and Dragon's Tooth came into view, my confidence began to erode. A strange sensation crept over my scalp. Things didn't look quite the way I remembered. I pulled toward the right bank to stop for a better look, but there was no eddy and the big baggage raft handled like the Queen Mary. I struggled at the oars, fighting down panic as we were inexorably dragged in. As we passed the point of no return, I uttered my famous last words: "It's OK, Polly, there's only one way to run this rapid anyway."

By the time I realized that it was *not* OK, because there was no right-side run at this water level, it was too late to move left. There was only time to square up and hit the big house rock head on. The bow rode up the rock like a breaching whale. Polly did her levitating act, then at the last moment, turned and looked down at me with that unforgettable expression, a mixture of disbelief and reproach that asked: "Is this the run you were talking about?"

"Hang on!" I shouted, but Polly was no fool. She jumped ship. The next moment, I felt like a dachshund being sat on by a sumo wrestler, as Big Bertha and the personal baggage of 20 people came down on my head. Everything I had neglected to tie in securely—

frying pan, Dutch oven, my best sweater—answered the call of gravity and made a quick, one-way voyage to the bottom of the Klamath.

I struggled onto the overturned raft, calling frantically for Polly until I saw her emerge on the far bank, looking like a cat that had accidentally fallen into the family Maytag. Then I looked upstream just in time to see Alan's guitar emerge from the tail waves, having made a clean run down the left side of Dragon's Tooth. Soon the boat floated into an eddy, where it circulated slowly like a great, dead hippo. I lay on the capsized raft with my chin in my hands, surrounded by flotsam, thinking how unfair it all was. How could the only flip of my career have happened on the Mellow Klamath? What would Polly think of me now? And how in hell were we going to cook dinner?

As it turned out, we prepared dinner for 20 in a pie plate. Polly, despite her good judgement in leaping off a sinking ship, later made the inexplicable mistake of marrying me. And I learned my lesson at the hands of the river gods: Pride Goeth Before a Flip.

A True Story
from the
Himalayas

By: Broughton Coburn

Anxious and distracted, I gripped the table leg where I sat in a tea stall pigeonholed in Kathmandu's noisy and crowded central bazaar. I tried to concentrate.

A boy wearing rags patched on rags stepped from behind the counter and, balancing a trayload of milk tea tumblers, set a glass at an adjacent table. Then, he looked at me.

It was there. Something was crawling out of my nose.

The boy froze as if electrically shocked. Dropping the tray, he ran from the teashop, fleeing as from the curse of the Hindu demoness Kali, Shiva's wrathful manifestation, whose gaze alone can mortify armies.

So, it was real, after all. Reflexively, I leaped up and over the spilled and broken glasses, and found the boy half-crouched and trembling against the wall of a nearby building, burying his head into his folded arms.

"What did you see? What did you see?" I asked him intently in Nepali, wanting to grab him and shake out an answer, or sympathy perhaps. I felt as frightened as he. Shielding his eyes from mine, he ran from my voice, head down, arms pumping, through the alley and across the next street.

My thoughts raced, trying to piece together the chain of events. I prayed that the ordeal that began 18 days earlier in the American Peace Corps office in Kathmandu might at last be nearing an end.

* * *

Recently graduated from college, I was a Peace Corps volunteer posted in Nepal, monsoon season, 1975. As I relaxed on the couch in the office lounge, reading my mail, a drop of blood splashed onto an aerogram from home. I looked up, unable to see where it came from. More drips appeared from my nose, bloodying my fingers. Not again, I thought—not an early symptom of yet another exotic Asian disorder.

I had recently returned from a trek to Mount Everest base camp. In my mind I reviewed the trip—the 18,000-foot altitude, the thin, crystalline air, the simple meals of well-cooked, bullet-resistant buckwheat pancakes, and the cold, refreshing mountain spring water. To drink untreated water at lower elevations, even if clear, would risk infection with hepatitis, typhoid fever, *Giardia*, amoebae and other parasites. But I disliked the taste of iodine pills, and a vigorous thirst could overcome my caution if the water looked as if it originated in a mountain spring. I had come to accept that, in Nepal, disease was an occupational hazard; and doctors, if available, often prescribed a shotgun treatment of broad-spectrum drugs. Risky place, this corner of Asia, I pondered while standing in the hallway, staring blankly at an outdated notice on the bulletin board.

Barney, the office doctor, stepped into the hallway. I said hello, but did not mention the brief nosebleed, afraid it might arouse too many questions. Barney was a pediatrician. Nepal, and tropical medicine, were new assignments for him. Each case he saw seemed to set off an imaginary beeper, allowing him to escape, scratching his head, to a medical text in his study. Generally, he would select an overweight volume, heft it onto the examining table, then read and reread passages aloud to his patients, becoming more indecisive with each rendition. The volunteers referred to him by the nickname of *"Ke Garne"* ("What To Do?") Barney.

Anyway, my nose had stopped bleeding. But when I bicycled through the bazaar to my apartment, it began leaking blood again, continuously, for 20 minutes. The next afternoon, I went to a tree farm to request seedlings for the village where I taught school. There, my nose dribbled again. Not knowing what to do, I held a handkerchief to my face like a shy, about-to-be-married Hindu woman hiding the terror and shame that she pictured awaiting her.

The following day, still bleeding, I saw Ke Garne Barney. He examined my nose with his nasoscope, and speculated that my nasal membranes might be weak, perhaps aggravated by the dryness and cold of high altitude. He gave me a bottle of neo-synephrine, a thumbs-up, a good handshake and a return appointment.

I gave the neo-synephrine a full trial, for three days, but from the first application, my nose only seemed to bleed more. Each day, it bled in painless, erratic spells. It dripped in the evenings, but not while I slept or, unaccountably, until 10 in the morning. I remained in Kathmandu, reluctant to return to the village where I was posted. Even without nose problems, to most villagers I was a strange enough apparition. I knew what they'd do with me: direct me to the shaman, who would likely deduce from a diagnostic trance that I had been infected by the hex of a witch with reversed feet, requiring that I shave my head and sacrifice a water buffalo to Narayan, an incarnation of Vishnu. Fine, but on my Peace Corps allowance I couldn't afford a water buffalo.

"Well, I might have to cauterize your nose," Barney suggested on the fourth day. "I can't think of what else to do." The neo-synephrine hadn't worked, and he could see no irritant.

"I'd like to wait," I told him, adding that I had heard that noses didn't smell as effectively after cauterizing.

"Well, yeah, I've heard the same thing," he shrugged in agreement.

Eight days of chronic bleeding. Rumors surfaced that Barney had misdiagnosed some patients, the positive side of which was that they got medically evacuated to Bangkok, a great place for overcoming homesickness. I needed another opinion, but during the monsoon, Barney was the only Western-trained doctor in town. Perhaps Warren, a scholar friend who lived downstairs, would have an idea. Warren's guru was a Buddhist priest of the Newar ethnic group, and the man practiced traditional Asian medicine.

On our Chinese one-speed bicycles, Warren and I threaded through the bazaar to the pharmacy and clinic of Dr. Mana Bajra Bajracharya. Descended from a 700-year lineage of Royal Physicians, Mana practiced Ayurvedic medicine, an empirical science described in the Vedas. It works by treating fundamental imbalances, rather than symptoms, by realigning the body's complementary elements of nerve, mucous and bile. Mana had earned a thick volume of testimonial letters from around the world—32 year's worth—extolling his cures for diabetes, hepatitis, arthritis, multiple sclerosis, sexual dysfunction and cancer.

Sitting in the waiting room, Warren assured me that Mana would have a safe and ready treatment. Aging but animated, the doctor appeared in the vine-framed doorway. He summoned me into his examining room.

Dr. Mana performed a thorough Ayurvedic exam, which included reading my pulse and turning my eyelids inside out, presumably to search for clues in the sound and pattern of blood vessels. Mana's diagnosis was similar to Barney's, but he was puzzled by the duration of the bleeding. He prescribed aloe, an herbal astringent.

That didn't work, either.

Fourteen days. The total loss of blood was not serious, but I began to question whether I would ever be normal again, as victims of chronic hiccups must feel, longing for rest. I wondered if I should have my nose cauterized, after all, or be evacuated to Bangkok or Atlanta's Center for Disease Control. Perhaps the village shaman should be sent for. I couldn't concentrate, saw fewer friends, stammered slightly, and experienced jarring flashbacks of college psychology case studies of deviants, and of cautions from the U.S. Government shrink who screened me in the United States. Long periods of isolation from that which was familiar, they all said, could induce hallucinations—or worse.

On the 18th day after the first nosebleed, I bicycled down a cluttered, medieval side street of the central market. Thankfully, my nose hadn't dripped in several hours. But from the corner of my eye, I thought I saw something emerge from my right nostril. I reached for my nose, which felt normal. I continued pedaling, presuming it to be a piece of coagulated blood.

There it is again. Then gone. *Yes, something is in there, and it's working its way out.* A panic flushed over me. My nose grew large in my field of view, and the world beyond my face diminished.

I needed to have this sighting confirmed by someone, by an earthling not yet infected. But if this thing was part of a generalized, insidious infection, I feared, people might not tell me the truth. I pulled over to a teashop, ordered a glass of tea and waited. Again I saw a blurred form, but felt nothing. That's when the boy in the teashop saw it, too, and at terrifyingly close range.

* * * *

Dumbfounded, I stood in the alley beside the teashop, watching the boy run off. I paid the startled shopkeeper for my tea, and the spilled tea and biked back to my apartment. In the bedroom mirror there was only a nose, a normal one. I drew up a chair and positioned myself squarely in front of the mirror, hands cupped on my knees, resolving to watch my nose until I saw it, the thing. For a quarter hour, self-conscious but purposeful, I focused, a hunter stalking himself.

Then, as if trying to catch me unaware, a long, brown, eel-like creature slid out, silently, offering no physical sensation at all. Guardedly, it scanned the air and retracted, leaving no trace. The probing tentacle of a monster. Kali. A hallucination, a mirage. I momentarily felt nonhuman, an alien sent to earth on reconnaissance to test the spiritual or intestinal fortitude of those who dared look at me. I would not last long in this incarnation. I would be captured for dissection by the world's scientific community.

"War-ren," I called haltingly. Warren ran up the stairs, perceiving from my voice a turning point. We met in the bathroom, where his initial skepticism turned to dread.

"Eee ... *Yaah!*" Warren exclaimed in unique, guttural sounds, appropriate for what we were beholding. He held his hands up, preparing to fend off the wormlike organism should it escape from me and head in his direction.

Experimenting, I found that, somehow, handfuls of water splashed up my nose drew out the animal a finger's length, weaving and searching. I tried to grab it, but was unable to touch it before it withdrew. Warren tried, his face distorted in trepidation and disgust, betraying his stoic military school training.

We couldn't even touch it. Our index fingers and thumbs were poised closely at my right nostril, but the slippery form retreated before either of us could pinch closed on it. Sensing any threat, the thing disappeared. We were horrified—Warren more than I; my hormones of self-preservation had overtaken the hormones of fear. So this was why I had found it strangely easier to inhale than to exhale through that nostril: the thing had formed a kind of a valve in there.

It was Sunday. Barney's day off. The American medical clinic was closed except for emergencies, which were discouraged.

"Let's go see Mana again. Now," Warren proposed. He was confident that Dr. Mana, though he missed the diagnosis, would at least recognize the thing itself.

We bicycled through a bazaar teeming with busy, unconcerned mortals. Like a Tibetan chanting his mantra, Warren rhythmically intoned, "I don't believe it. I don't believe it," synchronizing the don'ts to each pedal stroke. I repeated the familiar Buddhist mantra, *Om Mane Padme Hum*, but it came out sounding more like, "Oh, Mommy, take me home."

Mana motioned us into his study, an extension of his examining room. Demonic, cryptic charts peered from the tops of cabinets overflowing with unbound ancient texts. Glass cases lining one wall were filled with odd-sized, murky bottles of tonics with Sanskrit names. I thought I saw my name on one of the bottles. Mana said a few words in his tribal language to the gnomish compounder, who was wearing a smock caked with herbal and mineral—and what looked like animal—residue. He then turned to serve tea, assuming we had come to discuss a publishing project Warren had been helping him with. Warren stated that this meeting was of much greater urgency, then explained my situation. The thing was hiding. Perhaps it would burrow into my brain, or lay eggs. Ungraciously, Warren let out a spacious laugh.

"None of this is possible!" Mana interjected with customary confidence. "Thirty-two years I am a physician in Nepal, and I have *never* seen a worm in a patient's nose!"

I hadn't, either. "Watch this," I rejoined, equally confident, though my voice was breaking. I asked Dr. Mana to call for some water, and we stepped into his courtyard, a square of buildings that housed his herb stores, compounding his laboratory and the apartments of his extended family. His grandnephews and grandnieces ran about in carefree play until the compounder arrived with a glass. I squatted down. Mana and Warren followed. The children stopped playing.

I poured water into my hand and tossed it toward my nose. The thing came out on cue. Startling us, Mana jumped up, hands and fingers writhing, eyes rolling, face contorted.

"Aaahhh!" he cried, as if in anguish himself. "It's a *leech*!" A leech. A lurking, tenacious bloodsucker, evoking the quivering agony of Humphrey Bogart wading through a carnivorous, parasite-infested, uncharted African river—an animal that had found its refuge, a human host, where it could develop, mature, lay eggs, and finally emerge as an evolved, aggressive, and no doubt hungry, life-form.

Villagers had told me that leeches are inauspicious even by themselves, but by manifesting one in my nose I had been transfigured into an evil spirit of semihuman form. Even the children recognized it. Panic propelled them from the courtyard, running as if from a ravenous, multiarmed deity that subsists on small children. Women leaned from the courtyard's upper story windows and promptly latched the shutters, then climbed to the flat rooftops and called their neighbors to clamber over, across the roof—not at ground level—to see this from a safe distance. I felt a chill, and shivered uncontrollably.

Mana ordered tweezers, salt and more water, figuring that the salt, a good leech repellent, might cause it to release. We squatted again. I splashed saltwater into my nose. His tweezers could not touch the leech. He tried several times again. The saltwater only caused it to retreat further inside.

"I don't know what to do," he confessed, frustrated that the case had seemed to defy his entire Ayurvedic medical tradition, and in front of his family. "I give up. Maybe your Western doctor has some kind of suction machine." Genial in defeat, Mana desired only that it be removed any way possible.

I called Barney at home from the phone in Mana's waiting room. Excitedly, I described the events, though perhaps not in the order they occurred. Yes, a leech stuck its head out of my nose when I splashed water up it, but it always disappeared before I could touch it. I asked Barney what he thought. There was no response.

"Are you there?" I asked into the telephone. It was not uncommon for phone calls in Kathmandu to be disconnected.

"Yeah, yeah, I'm here." Barney didn't like surprises.

"Well, what do you think?"

"This is difficult. I don't know what to say, exactly, except that I ... I'd like to make an appointment for you to see the Embassy psychiatrist."

Ke Garne. I covered the receiver with my hand. Barney had decided that I was a drug- or culture-shocked deep end case—another not uncommon feature of Kathmandu. I needed someone to corroborate my story, a respectable witness. Mana was busy calming his extended family, who were peeking over the rooftops, worried about contagion; Barney would probably figure Mana as a quack, anyway. Warren, a long-haired, unemployed U.S. Air Force Academy dropout, might not qualify, but he occasionally did construction work under contract for a branch of the United Nations.

"I have a U.N. contractor here, his name is Mr. Warren Smithson, and I'm going to put him on," I said resolutely to Barney.

Warren was low on patience with any kind of authoritarian figure, which for him included American-trained professionals. He tried to turn the case around on Barney, asking if maybe he was nuts, reminding him that this was reality, that I had better get some respect, and that he had better know what to do about this, and do it soon. I reached for the receiver, fearing Barney might have us both carted off to the psych unit.

"OK, OK," Barney relented. "So, what do you want me to do about it?"

What To Do. "I want you to take it out," I tried to say calmly, though my tone was of exasperation and pleading.

"How?"

Barney knew of no precedent for a nose leech. Maybe his liability insurance wouldn't cover an untested leech removal procedure. I relayed Mana's suggestion about a suction apparatus.

"I'll think about it on my way down to open up the clinic," Barney offered. "But I can't promise anything ... I think the nurse should come, too, for this one," I could hear him add in an aside to himself.

Wearing the reluctant expressions of first-year anatomy students just introduced to their cadaver, Barney and the nurse greeted me with simple nods in the driveway of the American medical compound. Barney mumbled about not having been taught anything about this in medical school, of vacation time, and of his chances for getting transferred to a post in Europe or the tropics. He kept glancing at his beeper hopefully.

The nurse and I helped him set up the nasogastric suction pump, but the motor wouldn't operate: a burned fuse, with no replacement. Barney asked the two of us, for lack of specialists to confer with, if the pump would logically be the proper tool, and how he might use it if it did work. We had no idea.

I sat on the examining table. Barney inserted the nasoscope but saw nothing, hoping out loud that maybe the leech had fallen out while I was bicycling to the clinic. He flicked his head as if shaking off a dream, then brushed his hair back slowly and tightly with both hands, momentarily smoothing the set lines of his face. He fished out a pair of hemostats, resigned to having a go at grabbing it, just as Warren, Mana and I had tried.

I palmed water into my nose. I could tell that the leech appeared when Barney's body jerked. He hesitated, then bit his lower lip and approached, cautiously, as toward a dormant beast. Wait. Silently emerge. *Clamp*. Vanish. Wait. Emerge. *Clamp*. Missed again.

"Damn," Barney swore forcefully, as awed as the nurse and I by the lightning reactions of the primitive animal. Slowly, he backed away, as if trying to determine whether time was critical, or if he should stop right there and phone someone for advice, or maybe step out for a cigarette.

Sweating, his hand unsteady, he advanced again and tried clamping—randomly—below my nostril. After several minutes, he nabbed the end of the leech, the head, on its way out for air. He cinched down the hemostats' miniature grippers, and there the two of us paused, locked together in suspended animation. Then, with one palm on my forehead, he began to pull, slowly increasing the pressure. My focus narrowed as, cross-eyed, I watched the leech stretch outward. For the first time I could now feel the thing— pulling vaguely from the interior of my head, indeed as if from the back of my head. It wouldn't let go.

"Let me know if it hurts—otherwise, I'm ... I'm just going to keep pulling until something happens," Barney stuttered, sounding unsure of what that something might be, or whether he was doing the right thing at all. He now needed two hands on the hemostats. I braced one foot and a hand against the sidewall of the examining room, while my other hand gripped the back of the cushioned table to keep from being pulled forward. The leech was stretched out nearly a foot; again we hesitated in this position, braced. I could see Barney soberly trying to reckon that under prolonged, static tension the leech might loosen and release, though his face was twisted in anticipation of a horrible accident.

My neck strained against the pull. I heard myself mouthing Warren's mantra. *I don't believe it.* I realized that I might never again experience this, nor again see such an expression on a doctor's face. I had been told to expect the unusual in this country, but this was more like some altered, metaphysical dream. *I don't believe it.*

Something snapped. Barney hit the wall directly behind him, while I fell over backward across the examining table. I couldn't see where the leech went, if in fact it came out, or if it had taken part of me with it. I wasn't sure Barney knew, either, until, with deliberation, he held up the trophy—a fidgeting, clean, unattached leech, tightly seized in the clamps. Unstretched, it measured four inches long, as thick as a pencil, with a nickel-sized sucker on the host end. Barney's mouth hung open, grinning at the same time. As far as he could tell, he had done the right thing.

My nose dripped not a drop of blood. The leech, the hex, was gone. I said thanks and shook hands with Barney—still speechless—and stepped from the clinic to again join the world of benign, unencumbered humans. I slowed as I passed a neighborhood shrine. A gathering of devout Hindus were chanting, entranced, conducting a propitiatory ritual. I wondered if they had seen visions as gripping as my real one.

* * * *

Two days later I went to see Mana. He caught sight of me before I crossed the threshold of his clinic.

"I know how we could have gotten it out!" he declared buoyantly from his waiting room. "If we had held a glass of water to your nose, and kept it there, it would have dropped off into the water on its own. Yak herders attract them from the nostrils of their yaks that way. Your leech had completed a stage of its life cycle. It was done living in the host, which is usually livestock, and was waiting for a stream to drop into and float down, to reproduce and continue its cycle! Ha! You must have picked up the leech by drinking water from a stream the way a cow does!" He laughed loudly, unreservedly. I could feel the people sitting in the waiting room gawking at me with open, uneasy concern.

Then I remembered the mountain spring water. I had intentionally drunk on hands and knees, face in the stream, thinking it more sanitary. Of course. Villagers drink spring water from cupped hands, I now realized, to look for and avoid leeches.

I returned to the American clinic to tell Barney. He was preparing a small shipping box for the creature, which was now safely restrained in a stoppered test tube. He was intrigued by Mana's explanation of the leech's life cycle, and said he would inquire about the removal technique in a cover letter to the Smithsonian Institution, where he was sending the specimen.

I expressed some apprehension. "But if our leech is lost in shipment, no one will believe the story."

"I don't think they'll believe it in any event," Barney responded as he carefully lettered a small label. I could see him grinning to himself, as if listening to the sound of his name being announced at a tropical medicine conference somewhere in Europe or the Caribbean. The label he prepared read simply, "Nose Leech. Nepal." I was grateful that my name, and I, were not attached to it.

King Kong Comes to Wabag

By: John Long

D.B. looked confused as he pointed to a blurb headlined with: "Two Die in Enga Fight." I grabbed the newspaper and skimmed the story: "Two men died of ax and arrow wounds on Friday after a fight broke out between Lyonai and Kundu outside of Wabag, in Enga Province. Joseph Yalya, 38, of Pina Village, died of an ax wound to the neck; and Tumai Tupige, 39, also of Pina Village, died from an arrow through the chest. Police said about 800 men were involved in the fight. The fight broke out when Lyonai tribesmen accused the Kundu clan of using sorcery to kill a Lyonai elder."

Two casualties seemed rather modest for an 800-man brawl, but this was Papua, New Guinea, which some say God made first, when his technique was a little raw. Since every production resembles its creator, it follows that God is both insane and a genius, for everyone, natives included, stumble around Papua in a sort of daze, half astonished, half bored. D.B. and I had gone there strictly for the hell of it, looking for novelty, and were presently licking wounds after a nine-week exploratory thrash down the Strickland Gorge. We'd had a rough go of it, but after two days kicking around Mount Hagan in the remote Highlands, we were jumpy for another epic. Our flight to Sydney and then on to California was leaving in eight days, so it would have to be a quick one. Fact was, we'd worked and scrimped and had flown to the far side of the globe, had hacked down that hateful gully all those weeks to stumble out the ass end with little more than dysentery. But one look at that newspaper article and our prospects brightened.

We snagged a ride from Solomon Chang, a crazy, high-strung engineer of Chinese/Papuan parentage. Chang was driving to a reservoir project at road's end, 20-odd miles past Wabag, and wasn't expected there till the following day. The road, known as the "Highland Direct," was straighter than the Oregon coastline, but rockier; and this gave Chang nearly five hours to ramble on about native "warfare."

"The buggers spill onto the road sometimes," Chang said, "but they'll usually stop for cars. Maybe bum a smoke or two. And I've never seen them fight through lunch neither."

So there was more than a few histrionics to this warfare, though, according to Chang, somebody eventually had to die "to preserve the honor of the contest."

We had a solid week to get into trouble. Chang only had that night, but liked his chances. However, when we wheeled into that verdant toilet known as Wabag, we were disappointed not to continuously duck a salvo of spears and arrows. Rather, the same old routine: Kanakas dressed only in "ass-grass" (a thatch of kunai grass in front and back, secured with a leather belt), with axes over their shoulders, feathers or boar tusks through their septums, and as always, every jowl bulging of betel nut and rancorous red spit. We were right back to swatting mosquitoes again. But our boredom was nothing compared to Chang's.

"Look," Chang said. "We ferret out some chief, thrash his ass and make off with his daughters." He considered for a moment. "Better yet, his pigs. That'll get the machetes flashing."

D.B. stressed the need to proceed cautiously with cultures we didn't understand, and Chang said: "Oh, enough of that travel guide suet. I was born here, for Christ's sake." There was a long silence— not counting the truck bottoming out several times in potholes—and

I could almost hear the gears grinding in Chang's head. "OK. It's Saturday. We'll swing by the bar, then hoof it over to the theater for *King Kong Meets Godzilla.*"

"Followed by Vivaldi's Opus No. 6 played on bamboo instruments, I suppose," D.B. said. Wabag didn't even have a store, so I was with D.B. in doubting this talk about it having a theater.

"I'm on the square here," Chang insisted. "It's been Kong and Godzilla every Saturday night for two years. But it's not the flick that's the draw, it's the Kanakas. Most of them think they're watching a documentary. I've seen them hike in all the way from the Gulf Province to see it."

We checked into the Wabag Lodge, an open-air dive with running bath (the river), then headed for the bar. No Hard Rock Cafe, this was a cage of double chain link, with a cashier and a stock of South Pacific Lager inside. We paid first, then the beers were slid through a little slot in the chain link. We hammered down a couple, then made for the theater, following a dark path to a small clearing in the otherwise impenetrable thicket.

The "theater" (the Wabag Ritz, as Chang called it) was a converted cement garage previously used to store Wabag's three old John Deere tractors. A noisy queue of Kanakas passed slowly through the tiny entrance. Dressed exclusively in ass-grass, they were obliged to check in their axes and machetes, receiving a numbered bottle cap to reclaim them. Several men, newcomers to the Ritz, were confused by this procedure, but were quickly pacified by an enormous native official at the door. He, too, wore the ass-grass, but also a creased khaki shirt and a red beret on his billowing bouffant. He flashed a wide smile when he saw Chang.

"Sainaman tru." This from the giant.

"Strongpela tru," Chang came back. The two exchanged a five-move handshake, then Chang turned toward D.B. and me. "Dispelas em i pren bilong me. Americans."

"Oh, how ya doing?" the giant said fluidly. "You blokes best grab a seat while you can."

We went in. One hundred and fifty natives were already pressed inside. Several benches were in place, but most Kanakas chose to squat in the oily dirt. The front wall was whitewashed. The ancient projector sat askew on a bamboo stand. The heat was withering, but the aroma could have turned the stomach of a granite statue. The natives' diet is almost exclusively forest tubers and manifold shrubbery, and they continually pass a crippling wind, unabashed, and most sonorously. Blend that with knee-buckling body odor and the fetid stench of betel nut expectoration, then box it all in a ventless concrete sarcophagus and you have the Wabag Ritz.

"Swank joint, eh?" Chang chuckled.

"Probably no worse that the atmosphere on Mercury," I said. D.B. mentioned he was finding it just a little easier to breathe compared to when he had typhoid fever in Upper Volta.

"Pasim tok," the giant barked, and the crowd quieted. He flipped on the projector, which made a gnashing noise like someone feeding hubcaps into a wheat thresher. He compensated by turning the volume way up, which distorted the Japanese dialogue beyond anything human, but rendered King Kong that much more horrendous. As Kong stomped through Tokyo, swatting down skyscrapers and feasting on pedestrians, their legs flailing in his jagged teeth, dreadful shrieks issued from the mob, and many Kanakas dove beneath the benches, cowering and trembling and babbling about the "bikpela monki, em i kaikai saipan man."

During the scene when Godzilla and Kong had it out, a fight erupted in the corner. Just as a free-for-all looked a certainty, a torpedo-busted mother of six squealing kids swung her bilum bag of spuds upside a Kanaka's head, and all eyes returned to the wall. Later, a courageous Kanaka stole up to the wall to "touch" Godzilla. He turned around, squinting into the light, and was instantly bombarded by sweet potatoes and betel nut husks. He screamed, the crowd howled, the giant barked, and the bushman bolted back to his bench.

The end credits rolled out and the wall went blank. A short silence was followed by shouts for more. The giant yelled, "No gat," but the mob didn't buy a word of it, so to avoid a sure riot, he simply rolled the film back in reverse. As King Kong backpedaled through Tokyo, withdrawing reconstituted pedestrians from his snapping jaws and placing them back onto the sidewalk, great cheers boomed from the crowd. More farting, more yelling, more spitting.

Over the next six days we got to dance with "Queen Gigi" of the Highlands, all 200 kilos of her; were invited to dinner by the local police chief, and when we relished the tender meat, the chief told us we'd just dined on a stillborn boy and we believed him for two days. And at the party during the solar eclipse, D.B. drank so much raw cane liquor he passed out, and when I found him, a Kanaka was tattooing a cassowary bird on his back and had already tapped out the head—all but the beak. Then I got suckered into the Kanaka version of craps, involving thrown hornbill quills of different lengths. I'd won 40 kina, but kept losing and drinking and getting more pissed off. Finally I lost it all, two months' wages, to a toothless coffee farmer who kept his father's skull in a rusty powdered-milk tin.

But the queen and the chief's gag and even the tattoo all paled next to the feature presentation at the Wabag Ritz.

L'Adventure Du Parapente

By: Matt Akers Hudson

The village of Chamonix has long been a mecca for mountaineers the world over. My best friend Leo and I were there to test our metal on the icy cliffs of the Mont Blanc Massif. That was the theory at least. In practice, we spent most of our time flexing beer muscles and expounding on the doubtful nature of the weather. This left us plenty of time for lying about and staring up at the sky. We soon discovered hundreds of colorful dots circling the valley. As they descended, we could make out human forms arcing and gliding gracefully through the sky suspended by nylon parapentes. We were so taken with this sight that we vowed right then and there to try it.

Alas, the weather didn't cooperate. It was clear three days in a row, and we were forced to climb. When we returned from the hills, our meager budget was cooked, but our parapenting ambitions were still flying high. We beat a hasty retreat to Leo's house in the Pyrenees.

We arranged to take two days of flying lessons in the south of France. Speeding through the mist that perpetually hangs above the Pyrenees, we were soon past the border and heading down into France. We were nervous with anticipation as we pulled into the bar that was the headquarters for the paragliding guides. We were to meet a man named Patrice at 9 p.m. Ten o'clock came and went, but there was still no Patrice. We were beginning to have our doubts when a wiry unshaven man in a dirty pile jacket stepped into the bar. The barmaid informed him of our presence, and he ambled over to our table with a beer in hand. I was quite pleased to find he spoke passable English. He informed us that we had come at a bad time. After much negotiation, he finally agreed to take us out the next day with a class that already had some experience.

Our excitement was overflowing the next day as Patrice drove us through the French countryside in a beat-up station wagon. We drove on dirt roads through beautiful forests interspersed with green cow pastures. The rickety wagon switchbacked up a rugged dusty road and stopped on the shoulder of a large green mountain, where we saw a wind sock well extended in the breeze and several paragliders laid out on the grass. We walked a short distance and looked down into the valley. There was a checkerboard of forest and cow pastures 3,000 feet below. The cows in the pastures looked like ants. It was a long way down.

Patrice gave us paragliders and showed us how to lay them out. He strapped himself in and shouted instructions to us as he ran into the wind and pulled the paraglider up over his head. It seemed quite effortless as he pulled on the steering toggles and ran down the gently sloping hill. Next, it was our turn. I buckled into my harness and, on Patrice's command, ran down the hill raising the elevator straps above my head. I was promptly jerked off the ground and slammed into the turf. This wasn't going to be easy. Leo didn't fare much better, he took a nice 30-foot digger. After about eight attempts each, we could get the canopies over our heads about half of the time. Patrice gave us pointers when he wasn't busy helping other students launch off the 3,000-foot mountainside. We were more than a bit surprised when Patrice said to us with a curious grin, "We watch them, then you go."

I knew exactly what he meant, but still found myself saying: "What? Where? Off that cliff!?"

Patrice nodded and a sense of doom descended upon us. After less than an hour of training, we spread our paragliders on the yawning brink of what now looked to be the Grand Canyon, only bigger. We watched the other students, one by one, as they got clearance from Patrice and ran full bore into the abyss. They would run 10 or 15 steps before they would have enough speed to be lifted from the hillside and begin their flight. Flight instructions would come up on the radios shortly after takeoff. The ground man was just a speck in one of the pastures below. The instructions were all in French, but I could see that for each time the ground man gave an instruction, the pilots would make a corresponding turn. This continued until the pilots were lined up with the pasture where the ground man was standing. Just before they came to the ground, we would hear lots of instructions and the person would land. It looked just the same as we had seen in Chamonix.

One student wasn't so lucky with his takeoff. He was running down the hill and got his canopy a bit out of square with the wind. The resulting crash didn't look like it was any fun at all. It reminded me of someone being dragged across a meadow by a pickup truck at 25 mph. The man got up, dragged his chute back to the top of the hill and grinned as he laid out his paraglider for another attempt.

Next, a more experienced student took off and was hotdogging his way down, doing fast 360-degree turns. He made his final approach to the landing field and found himself a little short. Rather than deal with the trees surrounding it, he wisely chose to head for another pasture. The only problem was that this new pasture was full of cows. The poor guy barely missed hitting a steer and thought he was safe when he hit the ground. This was not the case; the man hadn't counted on his canopy coming down on top of the steer. The startled animal ran the length of the pasture with the paraglider hooked over his horns, and the unlucky student in tow. Patrice howled so hard with laughter that he fell on the ground while yelling, "Toro, toro, toro," and waving an imaginary cape. I didn't find it quite as amusing, knowing that I would be flying in a matter of minutes.

Patrice volunteered no information about how to steer the chute or land it, saying only that the man on the radio would tell us. Eventually we pried a basic flight pattern out of him and learned that we would slowly pull the brakes down to our sides when we were about 15 feet above the ground. Armed with this meager bit of knowledge, it was our turn to fly.

Leo would go first. The man on the ground spoke Spanish but not English. The idea was that once Leo was on the ground, he could translate the instructions for me. Leo got the signal from Patrice, hesitated for a few seconds, then went for it. A stream of vile obscenities rolled off his tongue as he bounded down the hill and parted company with the earth. Leo's flight came off without a hitch; and he almost landed on his feet. No problem. Now it was my turn. Serious butterflies were attacking my stomach and it took just about all the courage I had to run down that hill. The feeling was incredible as I gathered speed and began to increase the distance between my strides. Three feet, 6 feet, 10 feet, whoosh ... I was flying! The sound of the air rushing past my ears was incredible as I reached up for my steering toggles. The first thing I heard over the walkie-talkie that was strapped to my chest was a French voice. Soon this voice was replaced by Leo's reassuring chatter. He was giving me instructions in a clear steady voice.

"Go a little to the left. More, more. Good. Now go straight." The paraglider responded beautifully. As I pulled down on the left toggle, I gently spun to the left. "OK, Matt, go straight, straight, keep going." I was just beginning to enjoy the ride, when I looked down and noticed that I was a considerable distance from the landing area and heading away from it. Leo's voice was still very clear and calm saying, "Go straight, go straight." I was thinking, this is my first flight, I must not be able to judge distances very well. I was getting lower. I noticed I was over the trees. Still I could hear Leo saying, "Go straight, go straight." This was the voice of my best friend, the same person I had trusted my life to hundreds of times while climbing. I glanced down and knew that something was wrong. The treetops were only about 300 feet below me now. The radio went silent and a horrified glance over my shoulder revealed that I was out of sight from the landing area. The trees were getting closer and my mind raced. I had about 15 seconds to react or bite it. I spotted a small clearing on a hill. Jerking my left steering toggle hard to my side, I arced sharply to the left, clearing the treetops by no more than 40 feet. The ground rushed up to meet me. I thought, tuck and roll, as I pulled desperately down on my toggles to brake the chute. Slam! I impacted the hill.

I applied the brakes too violently and too late. After rolling on the ground and trying to regain my wind, I checked for injuries. Expecting at least broken bones, I was amazed to find myself mostly intact. A twisted ankle and some harsh bruises were the extent of my injuries. I felt like Chuck Yeager as I gathered my paraglider and limped back toward the landing area. A few minutes later, Leo got through to me on the radio and confirmed that I was uninjured. A farmer thought I was very curious looking. He laughed to himself when he saw my mud-stained clothes as I hobbled past his house cursing violently.

I met Leo coming up the road. "What the hell happened?" I screamed in an adrenaline-fortified rage. Leo explained that the ground man had been giving him instructions in French instead of Spanish. It turns out that the French have a nifty way of using the word "*droit*" for "right" and for "straight." Drawing only on his high school French classes, Leo had misinterpreted the instructions. The ground man was actually saying, "Turn to the right," but Leo was understanding, "Go straight." To compound the problem, Leo was holding up his right hand and pointing straight with it to be sure the instructions were correct. The problem was that the ground man saw Leo's right hand and assumed he meant, "Go to the right."

As I sat in the back of the dusty wagon for another trip up the mountain, I began to have serious doubts about my sanity. Just a few minutes ago I had nearly died, and now I was heading back up for another jump. What was wrong with me? Were my instincts of self-preservation somehow faulty? Had I gone off the deep end? Maybe I just had something to prove. This time, Patrice would be the ground man, and I would get by with Spanish instructions.

If it was hard to motivate myself the first time, this second jump would be twice as hard. When my turn came, I went for it and flew like a bird. No shit! There I was ... again.

A 5.9 Climber from Out of Town

By: Kipp Campbell

Soul said go on, Mind tried to determine how to go on, and Body was all for stopping. These three, this Soul, this Mind and this Body, are collectively me.

How do you do?

We're fine, thank you.

I've often thought that relationships would be so much easier if, when first meeting someone, one would inquire, "How is your soul today?" Then, "How is your mind?" And finally, "How is your body?" This would encompass such things as being happy or sad, being horny, not being horny, being victimized by a virus or coping with the monthly menses. Unfortunately, many people cannot begin to understand the concept of soul, much less inquire as to its well-being. I've often thought of the soul as the part of a person that does not die, the part that causes us to struggle, the part that gives us the spark of life and the ability to enjoy that life. Most of us can understand a sick or disarranged mind, and everyone knows what it's like not to feel well.

I'm thinking of all of this while standing on a rock ledge a long way up the side of a mountain. Now the climb I'm doing is not "technically" difficult, only 5.7 or so. While sitting in a bar with friends a few nights ago, I loudly stated, "Hell, I can climb any 5.7 made." Other factors enter the picture, however, here on this ledge, like, you're a father ... fathers are supposed to be there for their children ... fatigue, it takes a helluva lot of work to get this high up ... fear, that raw-edged emotion that you must work so hard to keep in check or it will overtake you, and if it overtakes you, your ass will be in much worse shape than you are in now.

I begin thinking about the various parts of me described previously. It occurs that I have no place to put fear. It obviously doesn't reside in my soul though another emotion, joy, does. It can't reside in the mind because my mind is a computer, it figures things out, it doesn't feel. My body feels the effects of fear, the sweaty palms, the grinding ache in my stomach, but fear doesn't reside in my body. I need a place for fear. How about my left ass cheek? That's a good place for it. Sure it is in my body but an isolated part.

This foregoing chat in my head causes me to smile slightly and fear is placed back and to the left, where it belongs. Nice to provide your own entertainment.

This climb is in the Canadian Rockies on a smallish mountain called Chinaman's Peak. I need to clarify here that a coal miner of Chinese descent named Ha Ling first climbed this mountain in 1886, hence, the name. The fact that this individual's first ascent did not receive formal notice speaks to our forefathers' (mothers'?) inherent racism. Therefore, instead of Ling's Peak, it became Chinaman's Peak. It is also not recorded whether this person of Chinese origin went up the clifflike north face or the more sloping, but still steep, south side. However, Ha Ling did apparently climb it and so are we. We, in this case, refers to not only all the parts of me but also to a first-class lead climber named Bill. Bill has climbed Chinaman's Peak many times. Bill is also twice my size, 15 years younger, has a lot of experience and is, therefore, an excellent person to have leading, especially when you are a 5.9 climber from out of town.

The climb consists of 12 pitches, mostly of blocky ledges with a few hàiry moves near the top. We climb over a rib. My Lord! The mountain seems straight up and down here, a good 2,000 feet or more to the nice lake below. The lake looks like it's from one of those pictures taken from a mapping aircraft.

Prior to this last move over the aforementioned rib, I had been climbing, aware of only the next two or three moves, watching how Bill climbed and making sure he was safely belayed. I had not actually looked around, except in a vague sense, until now. It was difficult at this point not to pay attention to the large, empty space all around me because there was absolutely nothing around me except this little ledge I'm standing on. Therefore, my mind tells me with computerlike detachment, pay attention to the rock because that's all there is to hang on to. Mind then instructs Body to move in such a way so as to stay safely on the ledge while Soul enjoys the view.

Being second, or last in this case, as there are only two of us, is like being top-roped. Therefore, even if I bail horribly, I won't fall more than a few feet at most—provided Bill is paying attention.

I trust Bill implicitly. Funny how climbers trust each other so much. We have to, I suppose, since our very lives depend on each other. But you always hear stories, or read them, of climbers who trusted the wrong person or believed they could do something they couldn't do. The rubric "overestimated ability" comes to mind. Here my case seems quite the opposite. I have the ability and my trust is not misplaced, but something keeps pointing out to me that I am high on a cliff face and could possibly fall off. This something rather clinically adds that I would probably bounce off four or five outcroppings on the way down, but of course, I would be dead anyway, so it wouldn't really matter ...

I must stop this and look to two things. The reality that (a) I have the ability and (b) Bill is beyond reproach in the trust/paying attention department. I also need (yes, need!) to enjoy the total experience, the view and this perfect warm day in these magnificent mountains. This is food for my soul that is only pushing the edge enough to be satisfying.

I have accomplished something. I have overcome a normal human feeling, fear. It wouldn't be normal not to feel some fear up here. It wouldn't be satisfying if you did not feel that fear. If you didn't feel the fear and in some way overcome it, you would be less than you are at the top.

Later, I crawl over the lip and sit on the top. I feel free and complete and exalted. I have added to my self-esteem. I have proved to myself that I can do it.

I stay there just looking out and down, not thinking really. Bill keeps himself busy by putting gear in order. I offer him some Gatorade which he takes and then asks how I liked the climb. I tell him my Soul loved it, my Mind is planning what to have for dinner, and my exhausted Body wonders how it's going to make it to the car. Bill looks around, he smiles and says that the most important thing is my Soul. For sure.

Bad Times in the Boston Mountains

By: Ted Gearing

I don't know how long we had been there. Minutes? Hours? They all seemed to run together. All I knew was this day had seemed like an eternity. Here we were with nothing but sheer walls on either side of us and an incredible boulder garden (more like a boulder plantation) ahead. But we'd come too far to turn back. There was no choice but to proceed.

In the late 1970s, the headwaters section of Arkansas' Buffalo River, the section known as the Hailstone, was still a closely guarded secret of "locals." It's 15 miles of Class III white water was available only when heavy rains fell upon the Boston Mountains and filled the Buffalo's tiny tributaries to the brim. At that time, the Hailstone had been run by only a few canoes and kayaks ... never by raft, at least as far as we could ascertain. That was our goal. That's why we had come— to make the first paddle-raft descent of the Hailstone.

Spring had been unusually wet as storm after storm wreaked havoc upon northwest Arkansas. Bridges washed out. Homes, cars and cattle were swept away. It was a bad year for everyone, everyone that is except for the white-water community. Boaters rejoiced at the prospect of full streams and a long season. One Thursday in April, a big storm moved across the Boston Mountains and continued on into Friday. Now it was the weekend and here we were, loins girded for battle with the Buffalo. There was an eeriness in the atmosphere and I couldn't quite put my finger on it, even as dark clouds tumbled over the horizon and even more bad weather began to brew. The effects of the storm season were startling. Old landmarks were gone. Nothing seemed familiar. It started to rain.

We were all tense. Everything had changed so much. We stopped when we could to scout what lay ahead. But, all too often, scouting was impossible and we would just have to "Go for it!!!" ... bouncing from boulder to boulder, hole to hole. We were lucky, very lucky. Then ... our luck ran out.

Rounding a turn, we were confronted by a fallen mammoth, a sycamore tree nearly five feet in diameter and stretching clear across our path. It was too late to stop. By instinct alone, we moved to the right, slipping through an almost imperceptible slot. We hit something, something sharp. We heard the unmistakable PSSSHHHHHHH of escaping air. But there was no place to pull over. No place to stop. We were on a downhill slide, nearly out of control.

We slammed into a boulder, then crashed through another hole, then another. Before I knew it, we were into a blind turn. Then it was up, over and down into the hole of all holes. We were engulfed by dark, muddy water. I was nearly paralyzed by fear. All around me were terrified faces. Bodies bounced about in the turbulence.

Confused thoughts rattled around my brain: "Is this the end? Did ambition overpower good sense? They were counting on me! What have I done?! What can I do???!!!"

There was but one answer. Only one thing to do ... put it in four-wheel drive and make everyone get out and push. What a mess! But after 30 minutes of grunts, groans, horsepower and manpower we were able to extricate ourselves. We changed the leaky tire and moved on. Another quarter mile of muck and goo, and we were at the put-in.

We never ran the Hailstone that day. By the time we arrived there was not enough daylight left. We spent the night at the river's edge as the clouds cleared and the water dropped to a level that couldn't be run. We sat around the campfire that evening, discussing the day's events. Were we disappointed that we hadn't gotten on the river? Hardly. For after one has run the Class VI *road* to the Hailstone, everything else really is ... just Class III.

Night and You and Blue Hawaii

By: D.V. Tyler

It wasn't as if I had never dived before; not like I had never strapped on a tank. No, this was an extremely embarrassing situation. I had to make a choice of being taken for a complete schmuck or dying a horrible death. But I precede myself.

Long before PADI or NAUI or any of those other organizations whose apparent purpose is to control the sale of air came along, I had been given a set of scuba gear by a large discount store, the result of a successful radio promotion. I thought that this would be a good time to learn to dive, so I drove out to Waimea Bay, put on the fins, tank, regulator and weight belt. I flippered over to a ledge near Shark's Cove and, since I have an aversion to any kind of personal instruction, jumped into the Pacific Ocean.

I sank like a bag of bolts, 30 feet straight down, and ended up sitting on the bottom, mesmerized. Waves were swirling over the ledge above me, and multicolored, aquarium caliber fish were swimming everywhere. The clear water faded to green in the distance, and the swirling white foam, where the waves met the ledge, created an audible and visible background for the scene.

Cool! It was one of the most beautiful moments of my life. I had been snorkeling and spearing fish since I was 10 years old, but I had never been this low, this long. After 10 or 15 minutes, I decided it was time to do something about getting back to the surface. It was obvious I would have to lose some weight, so off came the pieces of lead, one by one, until I began to lift off the bottom. I swam around a little, ignoring the amount of air in my tank. One of the few things I did know about diving was that you don't pop to the surface from anything below 10 feet. I slowly floated to the top, rode a wave over the ledge's edge and stood up.

That was the first of many dives to come. After that, I committed the Navy dive tables to memory, bought a life vest and considered myself a diver.

So how did I get in my present predicament, you may well ask. It all started when I married Marsha. She is one of the few women I have been close to who can keep up with me. Marsha has been beside me through volleyball, tennis, skiing, ocean and white-water kayaking, parasailing and more. She even gave racquetball a shot ("too noisy!"). And through it all, we have maintained a respectful relationship. Oh, sure, we regularly tear into each other, but it's the respect part that keeps us together. Anyway, when we were married, we decided that Marsha should learn scuba. I would no more teach my wife to dive than I would teach her to drive. Un-uh, under no conditions. So we signed her up for a NAUI-approved course. I couldn't wait. Not only would it be fun to dive together, but now I would be able to legally buy air. (I had learned to dive before any of the instructors' organizations existed. I refused to pay some kid with less underwater hours than me to teach me how to dive. There were no equivalency tests, so I had to have someone else buy air for me, like an underage kid hanging around a liquor store.)

Marsha's instructor, not aware of my outlaw status, invited me to join the group in its "ocean dive." The entire class walked out on a ledge on the right side of Hanauma Bay, jumped in and swam to shore. I joined the group, mainly for the beach party after the swim. It was fun, and Marsha received her certification. We should have stopped then.

A few weeks later, the couple we had been diving with (they had a boat) invited us to their dive club's monthly gathering. It was a group dive with about 20 people, a mile off Waikiki, at night. At night? It should be a piece of cake—everyone partners up, everyone has a light, everyone has a ball. Right. Picture 20 flippered, asthmatic, masked aliens in wet suits, shining lights in each other's faces and waiting to jump into the ocean. It was not a pleasant sight. When the boat reached the chosen spot, the crew dropped the anchor and fixed lights to illuminate the bottom of the boat and the first 10 feet or so of the anchor chain. Then it was everybody over the side, one at a time, of course.

I went about 10th, and hauled myself down the anchor line into one of the strangest spectacles I have ever seen. Everyone drifted off in a different direction, and beams of light shone everywhere. We had agreed that I would wait at the anchor for Marsha. This was the "buddy system," which, in Hawaiian waters meant that your chances of being eaten by sealife were reduced by 50 percent. The plan was for us to pair up with the other couple, and then we would all meander for a while, doing whatever was appropriate.

I waited on the bottom, shining my light into the face of each new arrival, completely unable to identify anyone, as each new diver let go of the chain and drifted away. I finally decided that I must have missed my companions, and that they were probably somewhere in the area. By now, the lights looked like an underwater version of a World War II air raid, with bubbles. When no more divers descended, I slowly swam away, taking care not to lose sight of the bouquet of lights below the boat. I had dived this area off Waikiki in daylight many times. Down to 160 feet or so, tidal waves, hurricanes and land development had turned most of the area into an underwater desert. Very few old coral heads and rocks remained. It could be pretty boring, so I opted to cruise close to the boat.

I swam around for a while, until I came up to an interesting rock face with a ledge that stuck out over the sandy bottom. I pulled myself over the rock and, upside down, peered under the ledge. It seemed open to the rear, so I flipped over and directed my light toward the back. I couldn't see the rear of the rock, but I knew that parrot fish sought safe havens like this in which to snooze. You can swim right up to sleeping parrot fish; they don't seem to react to the light until they're awake. They also seem to lose their balance ... sometimes listing about 45 degrees, just floating with the gentle surge. My favorite way to wake them up was to tickle them, which I had only done while free diving. Think of the surprise waiting for one of them down here!

I decided to swim deeper in. Farther back in the cave, a brilliant patch of blue slowly passed through my light beam. I pushed toward the back, my knees and elbows more useful than my flippers. Suddenly, a loud metallic clang from directly above me filled the little cavern, as the top of my tank whacked the bottom of the ledge. I scrunched down as far as I could and crawled on. Just a little more, and I should be able to see the fish, but my tank caught again, and, this time, my stomach did, too. The angle made it difficult to raise my neck to see straight ahead, and the back of my head kept hitting the regulator. I decided that was about it. Spooking a parrot fish was not worth this discomfort. I started slowly crawling out backward when my regulator jammed itself into a ceiling crevice that pointed toward the back of the hole. Coming in, it had slid past the rocky jut, just like a barbed fishhook, but it wasn't sliding out.

Crap! I tried to reach up over my shoulder to feel the situation out. The regulator had inserted itself up over a small, but solid, lip. I would have to crawl forward again to try and drag myself off the rock. At least that was the approach I had chosen ... when my light went out. That's right, my light went out. I have never seen such black. I have never heard such quiet. I have never felt so alone. That's right. No shit! There I was ... 50 feet underwater, 20 feet underground, wedged in a cave in total darkness with absolutely no idea how much breathable air I had on my back. I swear on a stack of *National Geos* that every word is true. That night I found myself in a position that would turn your hair white. (Yes, my hair is white.)

Now, I've been zapped by serious vertigo in high places; and I know how easily panic can build, until giving in to it becomes the easier alternative. That's how some people die. I knew that, and I also knew that, here and now, my life wasn't really in immediate danger. I had a few minutes to deal with the situation. Panic hadn't yet become a choice; the only thing I had to fear was fear, etc. But after 10 minutes or so of struggling to free the regulator, attempting to crawl forward and trying to get my light to work, I began to get a little uneasy. Nobody knew I was in trouble, and even if they did, they wouldn't have the slightest idea where I was. This was not only serious, it was becoming extremely unpleasant.

I hunkered down and intensely considered and discarded one option after another. Unfortunately, in that particular situation, there weren't all that many to consider, and, by the second option, I had run out. The only choice left was panic, so I started to kick the shit out of that rock. I shook my shoulders. I kicked my feet. I pushed back and forth as hard as I could, and lo and behold that rock gave! Gravel began to float around my neck and head and into my wet suit. I slowly pushed myself backward, steering with my feet. When I felt the water temperature change, I turned around. There in the distance was the welcome sight of many underwater lights. It was either the boat, or Captain Nemo holding a ceremony. I headed off toward the divers climbing the anchor chain. As I swam, I thought about dumping my useless light on the ocean floor, when I realized that now the damn thing was on!

There was such a crowd around the anchor line that I decided to surface and climb into the boat from the side opposite the ladder. There was a little floating seaweed on the water, but the swim was easy. When I reached the boat, I put one arm over the gunwale and hauled myself on board. I pulled off my flippers and walked aft where the others were coming in. As I made my way through the dripping throng, someone stuck their light in my face and shrieked! Suddenly lights from all directions were on me. There was a lot of noise, too, but I couldn't make out what they were saying. However, through my mask, I could see what looked like some of the seaweed wrapped around my head. I reached up to pull the stuff off, and someone yelled, "Don't touch it!" I was ushered to the very rear of the boat and a water hose turned on my head. The tips of my ears began to burn, and it dawned on me that I had surfaced, not through seaweed, but through a Portuguese Man-o-War, which was now festooned around my skull, right in front of my eyes.

It was becoming a night to remember. Fortunately, the boat carried meat tenderizer for treating protein poisons, so no one would have to whiz on my head. So I'm standing there, ears burning, but happy to be alive, when up flippers my still wet-suited, but sweet Marsha. Just in time, too, for I felt I had earned some big time comforting.

"Where the hell were you?" she hissed. "We waited at the bottom of the anchor line until we finally gave up. You could have been a little more considerate and waited for us."

I had no reply, as she flopped away in her wet suit, but you can bet, we've never been night diving again.

Geronimo

By: Scott Whitmire

My rookie jump partner had to shout in order to be heard above the loud hum of the turbine engines and the roar of the wind rushing through the open door at 100 miles per hour.

"Which end of the meadow are you aiming for?" he asked, with fear and trepidation etched across his face. The meadow he referred to was 1,500 feet below us and appeared to be the size of a postage stamp. The fact that it was surrounded by tall trees, some more than 150 feet high, did nothing to assuage his fears. He was supposed to be afraid, he was a rookie parachutist. I, on the other hand, was the "salty old fart," having jumped almost 100 times. I was a smoke-jumper, a wildland firefighter who parachutes into remote and inaccessible areas. Fear was not a part of my vocabulary.

So it was with a cavalier air of arrogance, cloaked in machismo and latent with stupidity that I shouted, "Just follow me," and launched myself out of the airplane and into the sky above the Sierra National Forest. The loud blast of noise which had been present inside the airplane was replaced with a silence so complete that I could hear the gentle sound of nylon rubbing against nylon. After a terminally long five seconds, I heard the distinct pop of my parachute opening, followed by the sound of my own breathing, deep and forceful.

For a brief moment in each jump, there is a feeling that can best be described as tranquil, that instant when relief gives way to a peaceful sensation of floating.

But my serenity was quickly shattered by what is every smoke-jumper's nightmare. Instead of flying over the soft and green meadow, I found myself drifting over rocks, trees and jagged cliffs, the likes of which have ended many a jumper's career.

Parachute manipulation is a difficult skill to master, as it requires focused concentration, an awareness of wind direction and a sense of depth perception. Screw up on any of these and the odds are good that that you will end up hitting a tree, landing in rocks or slamming into the ground like a giant lawn dart.

I screwed up on the first task, totally losing my concentration. Instead, I found myself gazing at the beautiful scenery of the magnificent Sierra Nevada mountain range. The San Joaquin River drainage unfolded below me, with sheer granite walls rising 200 feet high on both sides of the river. Thousands of acres of pristine forest lay before my eyes, resplendent with alpine lakes and towering mountain peaks. Majestic Balloon Dome captured my attention, looking like a smaller version of Tenaya, or Half Dome, its popular cousin to the west.

Therein lies the reason why I found myself well past the meadow with the ground and trees rising up to greet me like a giant flyswatter. Muttering obscenities, I tried to set up for a good landing by facing into the wind, which would soften my impact with the not-so-soft earth. Instead, I hit a huge cedar tree, with limbs which seemed to beckon me like a giant octopus.

Crashing through the upper limbs, I prayed that my canopy would hang up on the tree well enough to slow my fall to the ground. It did. I came to a halt 60 feet above the ground, swaying to and fro like a puppet on a string.

I glanced over at the meadow in time to witness "the rookie" settle softly into the center of the meadow, the target we were supposed to aim for.

From my lofty perch high in the tree, I marveled at his beginner's luck, then proceeded to rappel from the tree. This was a difficult task, made more so by the weight of my 60-pound jumpsuit and the flush of embarrassment I felt from having landed in a tree. I knew I would have to endure teasing and snide banter from the other jumpers regarding my tree landing, so I was already formulating a bombproof excuse for my shoddy parachute manipulation. Once safely on the ground, I yelled out to the other jumpers that I was OK, and I sank to the cool, soft earth in blessed relief.

Later that night, after we had put a line around the entire fire, we took a much deserved break to have some food and coffee by the warm glow of the campfire. Everyone took turns describing their individual jumps, as this is a smokejumper tradition, one which usually entails some exaggeration and the use of hyperbole to liven up the tales.

When the time came to explain my perilous tree landing, I felt compelled to tell my version with uncharacteristic veracity. Looking the rookie straight in the eye, I said: "There was only enough room for one parachute in the spot, and the damned rookie crowded me out, forcing me into the trees. He ran me out of the spot!"

Everyone laughed and accepted my version of the story as truth, despite his protestations, for I was the "salty old fart," and he, well, he was only the "rookie."

Slammed
on the Salmon

By: Mark Deem

I should have known. When the phone rang, and I heard Dave say, "Hey! Check this out!" I should have slammed down the receiver and beat it with a pipe wrench. But, as always, the combination of that voice and that phrase set off a chemical reaction in my brain which makes suicidal death jaunts sound like great fun.

This time, the plan was to join a group of similarly unbalanced individuals for a private raft trip down the California Salmon River (the Slammin' Salmon). A friend of a friend knew a guy who had a partner, and the two of them were starting a guide service. They were organizing this trip as a pilot run for the business and to get some action shots for their brochure. Three days of rafting Class V white water and peeing in the woods—sounded great! Never mind the fact that my river resume consisted of a one-day Class III lineup down some eastern backwater. Never mind that this was the biggest water season that California had seen in eight years. I'm an experienced outdoorsman, I figured, and besides, these guys are pros, right?

We pulled into camp and collapsed around 3 a.m., after piloting my old VW camper through 10 hours of rain, rock slides and winding one-lane roads. The next thing I knew I was gripped by a nightmare about a 5-foot troll who looked like he had been caught in a trash compactor, screaming at the top of his lungs.

"Wake the f@$# up, you bunch of limp d&#$, mother f#$%@ing sons-of-a-b*&%@#es!!!" Oh God! It wasn't a nightmare, it was our host, Peter, greeting us with his traditional wake-up call. This is a guy who, in his former life as an engineering contractor in the medical field, accidentally knocked out his own front tooth just before a presentation to a board of directors. He glued the tooth back into his mouth with industrial adhesive, then gave his proposal. Later, someone pointed out to him that he had glued the tooth in backward.

We slogged out of our wet tents to eat breakfast in a miserable gray drizzle and to meet our other guide, Rich. Rich never spoke, unless it was to say something negative and foreboding about the river. Breakfast consisted of Old Milwaukee and pancakes which, due to the lingering effects of my recent brain imbalance, tasted great.

The first day on the river was unbelievable. After carrying our rafts past others heading out ("Too high dude—too much rain!"), we spent a wild day on the river fighting for our lives. After the first two rapids, our raft was in sync with the river beat. With Peter screaming a stream of obscenities occasionally interspersed with paddling commands, we slammed our way through every rapid. They came and went so fast, we barely had time to set up for each new torrent. Rich's boat did almost as well, with the exception of a hellacious wrap-up on an 8-foot granite fin called ... The Fin.

We finished the day feeling like kings. That night, swilling beer, roasting chickens and howling at the moon, we gloated about how we had "danced with the river." And the river gods grumbled.

The second day of the trip turned into a rest day. Peter, Rich and a few other guys wanted to drive to town to watch the football game. The rest of us decided to raft the upper Salmon Bar section of Class III water with a full load of beer. We'd raft each section, beach the boat, then swim the rapids. At this young stage of my river career, I had no way of knowing how much we were pissing off the river gods.

Day three broke with the lightest gray skies so far. The river had dropped a lot over the past two days, so we were all psyched for a totally different run. All of us except Rich. Mumbling a mantra of, "We're all gonna die," he finally agreed to wedge himself back into his wet suit.

As we slithered back into our cold, damp suits, I noticed that Peter was sitting on his tailgate loading film into his camera.

"Come on ya' fat Czech," I yelled, "get into your suit!"

"F$#@* that!" he replied. "You candy-asses are gonna kill me! I'm stayin' dry and takin' pictures for the brochure."

After a lot of yelling and an unsuccessful coup d'état, my raft crew decided that Grant, who had rafted eight or 10 rivers before, would guide our boat, and to hell with Peter. Rich chanted his mantra, and we all headed for the river.

It was apparent from the first rapid that things had changed. The river gods were pissed. What had been jet-stream chutes two days ago, now showed jagged rocks a foot or more above water level. The river had dropped just enough to make the setups more technical and the holes more dangerous. This was soon proven by Rich, who, on the third drop, got pitched into a hole. Before he could roll into a ball and get shot to the surface, the river sucked the wet suit booties right off his feet.

The next near disaster hit at the infamous Freight Train rapid. Freight Train is a giant drop straight into a 90-degree bend bordered by a rock wall. As if this weren't enough, the set-up consists of an upriver drop aptly named Last Chance. You either set for both rapids at Last Chance, or you swim Freight Train. We made it, though, by the skin of our teeth—a five-man high-side barely saved us from being pitched onto the crowd watching from the top of the rocks. Rich's raft flailed through Last Chance, then started for Freight Train sideways. Waiting in an eddy below the rapid, we actually heard the crowd on the rocks yell, "Oooh!" as they spun toward the drop. Through some Herculean effort, the boys straightened out the boat just as they dropped into the Train. The gods had been cheated again.

There was no cockiness left as we regrouped in the eddies below the Train. We decided to take the rest of the river easy and get home alive.

At the top of the next rapid, we headed for a calm spot in the middle of the river. Rich's crew was about 50 yards upriver. As the boat was sucked into the faster current, we knew we had called it wrong. We were suddenly looking at the edge of the world as the front of the raft dove over the falls. Grant was rocketed into the back of one of the front paddlers, Ted, shooting him out of the boat. Larry's tenuous hold was ripped away by the huge standing wave in front of the falls, sucking him into the void. Grant, Dave and I high-sided for our lives. Wrong move. The wave spun us under the falls and flipped Dave into the curtain of water. As we spun back up the face of the standing wave, I stood up to dive for my paddle, just in time to see Rich's boat heading for the falls, ready to crush us in the pit. The last thing I did, before flying through the air and under the falls, was to wave them away.

Tumbling. Slow motion. Surrounded by green. Sounds muted. Millions of bubbles. Spinning slowly. Bumping something hard— the river cliff. Clawing at the rock. Fingers finding a crack. Green turned to gray and white. Icy water running past my eyes as the world spun into focus. The sound of rushing air. Inhaling it into my lungs. And then the terror-choked sound of Grant screaming, "JUUUUMP!"

I snapped out of slow motion just in time to see Grant alone in the raft being spit down the backside of the standing wave, clawing at the water with his paddle. He was heading straight for me, screaming at me to jump for the raft. Clinging desperately to the cliff face which penned the river, my only choice was to be squashed by the raft. So I jammed my foot against the rock, took a deep breath and dove.

The raft caught me at thigh level, slamming me into the cliff and knocking the wind out of me—again. Grant clawed at me crazily, trying to pull me into the raft. It seemed like an eternity of struggling before we realized that our last paddle was jammed handle first into my life jacket, holding me in the river.

We spun out of control through Class III and Class IV white water as Grant hauled me aboard, and we got the raft into an eddy. We eventually got everyone else aboard. Rich's raft had picked up most of our swimmers. Ted, however, was perched on a rock 20 yards upriver, where he had crawled ashore after nearly losing consciousness in the hole. It took us 15 minutes to calm him down and convince him that there was no way for us to reach him or for him to climb up the cliff. His only choice was to jump into the river again and grab for the rescue line. He made it aboard easily, but spent the last few river miles crouched in the center of the raft, arms locked around a center tube, close to tears.

"Just get me off the river! Just get me off this f*&#ing river! I swear I'll never touch water again!" Ted jabbered over and over, eyes so wide and wild that he looked like Marty Feldman on speed.

As we floated the last few miles to the haul-out, I surveyed our wreckage. We had lost three paddles, one rescue line, one helmet, two wet suit booties and most of Ted's conscious mind. It may have been the grating of our raft across the gravel bar, but I could swear that as we pulled the raft into the haul-out, I heard the river gods laughing.

A Bear Story

By: Andre Theisen

Having spent much of my childhood in northern Minnesota, bear stories were a regular part of growing up. Our cabin's kitchen windowsill had claw marks from an inquisitive cub, our garbage was occasionally raided by the beasts, and blueberry-picking efforts were often made more interesting by the presence of bear scat, with the fear factor proportional to the freshness of the droppings. My respect for the black bear did not peak, however, until an encounter on a canoe trip into Minnesota's Boundary Waters Canoe Area Wilderness.

I was leading seven boys on a weeklong summer camp trip with the help of my fellow counselor, Brad. Unfortunately for Brad, the trip happened to coincide with the peak of his misgivings about his impending marital state, which he was scheduled to enter just three short weeks later. Being banished to the wilderness with a pack of neophyte suburban brats did not exactly aid his mental stability. Nor did his rash decision to embark upon a complete fast—a decision prompted by the fear that he would not fit into his wedding tux, which had been unwisely ordered under the assumption that Brad's potbelly would not be attending the ceremony.

As the campers' whining and the lack of nourishment took their toll, Brad's despair increased, and he began to verbalize his doubts about marriage to no one in particular. By the third day, these musings had deteriorated into fairly incomprehensible rantings. In our tent at night, Brad's mind teetered back and forth, expressing sheer terror at the impending union one minute, then mushy longing for his beloved the next. At one point, he lay our route map across his chest, balanced his flashlight on his forehead, and called upon the "Great God of the Boundary Waters" to deliver him from the wilderness. I decided the best response to Brad's growing dementia was to ignore it, so I rolled over and managed to fall asleep while he babbled on.

In the early morning hours, I woke up to the sound of deep grumbling. I assumed it was Brad, in the throes of some love-inspired nightmare; but as my senses sharpened, I realized the noises were originating from outside the tent. I unzipped the back panel and exchanged stares with the largest bear I have ever seen in my life. He was comfortably perched in a red pine not more than 50 feet from our tent, sampling goods from our food pack. Not wanting to fumble around with the leather straps, the bear had simply sliced open the thick canvas pack with a swat of his paw. We had hung the pack there the night before, unable to locate a suitable tree farther from the campsite. The pack was 15 feet off the ground and a good 5 feet out from the trunk; but by clutching the trunk with his right paw, our visitor had no trouble exploring the pack's contents with his left.

Without breaking my stare, I woke Brad with the only vocabulary that had not deserted me: "Bear. Bear. Bear. Bear." Brad got up, exited the tent and roused the kids in a single motion. We gathered within shouting distance, several voices cracking from a combination of fear and puberty. But our breakfast guest paused only long enough to give us a disdainful nod. He had seen this approach before, and he was not impressed.

It was then that one smart-assed kid from California, who had appointed himself "Wilderness Expert" at the outset of the trip, declared that the correct method for dispersing such intruders was to bang pots together. When he grabbed our two frying pans to demonstrate, the bear snorted with obvious displeasure. The lame attempt to shout him away was one thing, but this kid with the old bang-the-pots routine was clearly more than he would tolerate. He knocked the pack to the ground and began to descend the tree. In one graceful leap, we were in the canoes and out on the lake. We watched respectfully as the bear sat on his haunches and snacked on our supplies, occasionally snorting his disgust at our decidedly lowbrow approach to camping cuisine. Eventually frustrated by the more complicated containers, he cursed his lack of opposable thumbs and lumbered off into the bushes.

With no alternative, we returned to the campsite and hastily packed up our tents and gear, unsure of just how far back into the brush our friend had gone to digest our breakfast. When everything but the food pack was loaded and ready to go, Brad and I flipped a coin. One of us would have to retrieve the pack. I lost. I ran to the pack, snatched it by the leather straps, and sprinted back to the canoes in terror, fully expecting claws to shred my flesh at any moment. I leapt into my canoe, amazed to find all my limbs still attached. A whoop went up from the kids. We inventoried our losses and decided we could still complete the trip as planned with the food that remained. We were about to resume our journey, when Brad realized our medicine kit was missing. In addition to first-aid essentials, it contained the California kid's daily medications for hyperactivity. We had to find it.

Brad and I reluctantly returned to the campsite again and gingerly disembarked. We spotted a corner of the white Tupperware box that served as our medicine kit, back in the brush—20 feet from where the food pack had sat. Out of earshot of the kids, I bravely suggested to Brad that since I'd gone for the pack, it was only fair that he go for the kit. He agreed, and tensely tiptoed toward the Tupperware. Just as he bent down to snatch the box from the ground, a black snout emerged from the bushes to his left. Brad froze with his fingers on the box, the bear only 10 feet away. Something like a whimper escaped from Brad, and then he smiled. "I'm getting married," he told the bear. Their staring contest continued for a moment, then the bear snorted, tucked its head and wheeled off through the brush.

As we paddled away from that campsite for the third and final time, Brad stretched his arms skyward and offered a prayer of thanksgiving to the "Great God of the Boundary Waters."

First
Halloween Run

By: Chad LeDuc

Ever since I was first able to read, the romance of the far north has intrigued me. As a child, I would spend unending hours reading the works of Jack London and Robert Service, sitting by a fire and fantasizing about those hardy souls and their dogs as they braved the Great White Silence alone. I swore when I was old enough I would also have dogs and challenge nature's arctic forces like those brave men.

After I went away to college, the challenges changed considerably, and I found myself more engaged in the pursuit of the opposite sex than anything else. So after college, when a job opened up in International Falls, Minnesota, the proverbial "Icebox of the Nation," I was torn between my fantasies of youth and my fantasies of the fast life in the Twin Cities of Minneapolis and St. Paul. The Falls won out upon a drunken bet with my roommates; and in the fall of 1979, I packed my beat-up Datsun with all my worldly belongings and set out on my northern odyssey. The plan was to spend a few years living on the edge of civilization, then move back to the big city, after satisfying my "adventuresome" spirit.

Like everything else, my plans unexpectedly changed. I fell in love, not only with Brenda, but with the beauty of the Borderland. Now, 15 years later, I call northern Minnesota home, and I have no intention of leaving.

To do a musher, of course, I needed dogs; and the first one, a malamute pup, was acquired in early 1980. I lived in a small basement apartment in Littlefork some 20 miles south of the Nation's Icebox, so for that time, an entire team of dogs still existed only in my imagination. Sadly, the pup was killed by a motorist in the summer of 1980, but not before I really had chance to develop a healthy appreciation for the work and time involved in handling sled dogs.

It was some 11 years later in January 1991, after marriage, two kids and a move to a house in the country that I realized I still needed to embark on the adventures I dreamed of as a boy. It occurred when I took my children, Jaime and Charlie, for a "real" sled dog ride put on by the only musher in the area as part of a civic winter celebration. When they came back from their five-minute cruise, one look at their faces rekindled my old childhood fire.

I decided wisely to start out with just a few animals and so a week later, I came home with Yukon, a three-month Alaskan puppy, which the kids loved and over which the wife threatened divorce. It took only a few weeks of my sleeping in the garage with him, when Brenda accepted us both back into the house on the agreement that there would be no more pets. Agreements, however, are made to be broken, or something like that.

In any event, the next dog was a Canadian Eskimo pup we named Echo. She followed me home on my birthday on April 1, conveniently doubling as a present to myself and a practical joke on Brenda, over which she only became mildly upset. I explained to her that Echo wasn't a pet as such, but a means of transportation, and therefore did not technically breach our agreement.

Having sold that line, I recognized the opportunity, and a few weeks later, Makoosh, a tiny black Alaskan puppy, together with Sunny, his grandmother, mysteriously materialized in our yard. Brenda, at that point overwhelmed, conceded and the the team was formed. Problem was, the only experience I had with dog teams was in my imagination; but being undaunted and compulsive anyway, I quickly picked up two more dogs (Brenda still hasn't noticed) for a song and anxiously waited for snow.

When it came on Halloween, covering all the roads with five inches, I called Steve, the local musher, and proudly announced I would be taking my team of out for their first run in the morning.

"Great!" he said. "How many are you going to start with, one or two?"

"Right," I joked back. "I'm sure those six little 50 pounders probably won't be able to move my weight and my kids to the end of the driveway, but we'll see. I'll start out slowly, then build up to 15 or so dogs, I think." I should have taken his convulsive laughter as an omen.

So bright and early the next morning, with Jaime and Charlie bundled up in the sled basket, Brenda and I began harnessing and hooking up the dogs—all six. Brenda's first skeptical comment came when she suggested I only take three dogs for a starting run.

"Don't you think six dogs is a bit much to control?" she gasped from underneath the tangle of two of the wild, howling beasts.

"Nah, this is going to be a piece of cake," I confidently hollered back. "After all there is only 300 total pounds of dog, and with the sled, the kids and me, we almost outweigh them. Poor little pups probably won't even be able to move us. I'm sure I'll have to help them up the hill," referring to the 20-foot rise at the end of our drive.

Actually the drive rises 20 feet, traverses the crest of a hill, then drops 150 feet or so in the span of a quarter mile, emptying out onto Monahan Road where you can turn either right or left, 90 degrees.

"Don't worry about us, worry about the dogs. I'll probably have to carry some of them home," I said as I finished finally hooking up the last dog. "Just pull up the snow hook and help me push the sled up the hill. We'll see if the dogs can pull us for a ways after that."

So Brenda pulled the hook, and I was physically introduced to mushing. The sled jerked out from under me, slamming me to the road, but for some reason (instinct, I guess, from my years of reading Robert Service poetry), I had a rope tied to the sled and looped around my arm.

When we hit the top of the driveway, I figure we were going between 15 and 20 miles per hour. We would have been going faster, but my torso was serving the purpose of a human brake.

All I could hear at that point was the drumming of 12 pairs of canine feet, my kids giggling and screaming, "Faster, Daddy, faster!" and my futile muffled, "WHOAMFFFF," as I ate snow and struggled in vain to climb out from underneath the sled.

Actually the ride, thus far, was comparatively mundane. It got exciting when I finally climbed back onto the runners just in time to start down the 150-foot hill. The sled no longer had me for a brake, and when we reached the halfway point down the hill, I know we were going 40 miles per hour. We began slowing a little bit after that when the sled started creeping up, sideways and parallel with the team, who were sprinting for all they were worth. I swear as we pulled alongside of them, I could see them smiling.

One thing I found out about going down a hill sideways on a dogsled is that you completely relinquish what little control you might ordinarily have to gravity.

So we were totally out of control at 30 miles per hour when we hit Monahan, and I mean, we hit it big. I, of course, was out of my mind with fear, screaming, "Whoa! Halt! Stop!" and a few other choice expletives. I didn't realize at that time that such loud activity from the back of the sled to untrained dogs was like cheering a sprinter across a finish line.

The dogs decided, with the uniformity of a formation of Canadian honkers, to take a left onto Monahan, which was real bad since at that point the sled was pointed right. It snapped around, and the effect on me was like being at the end of a skaters' crack-the-whip line, as I was rocketed into the trees on the opposite side of the road.

I lost it at that point. My little babies were still in the sled, which in my mind had taken on a werewolf persona dragging them to certain doom. I tore my way back up onto the road, expecting to see the whole works disintegrate into another dimension (or at least disappear around the curve at the end of the road), but, lo and behold, the dogs had stopped!

The kids were hysterical with laughter, the sled was on its side and the team was standing there with these shit-eating doggie grins, looking back over their shoulders mocking me. I was apoplectic, shaking violently as I ran to the sled, but when I was less than a foot away, the kids yelled, "Go," and the whole darn thing (on its side) took off again without a driver.

"You kids bail out, jump, roll out of the sled!" I wailed, and surprisingly, they both obeyed in unison, giggling and wrestling like a couple of cubs. I flew past them toward the sled, and as I did, gasped, "Good kids, go get mama quickly," thinking I'd stop the dogs and get her to help turn them back toward home.

I can tell you now that to a musher, there are no feelings more sinking than sprinting all out to your sled, only to watch it get smaller and smaller as the dogs widen the gap between you and them. By the time I got to the next junction of Monahan Road and Gold Shores Drive, they were gone, nothing more than drag marks and footprints. My only hope was that, with luck, they'd tire before they got to the highway.

Why I felt that luck was a possibility, with everything else that fouled up, is a mystery. In any event, I reached State Highway 11 about 30 minutes later, looking like a novice skier wearing a flannel suit.

My buddy, a local realtor nicknamed J.R., was just happening by, and one look at his mirthful countenance told me he had seen them. His window rolled down, and he said, between chuckles, "They're at Tilson Creek, headed to town going 90 miles an hour down the middle of the highway."

At this point, I got religion. "Please, God," I thought, "if they don't cause a fatality, I'll give this up and never do it again."

J.R. gave me a ride toward Tilson Creek, and miraculously the dogs had been stopped by a friendly motorist just past there, some five miles from home. I bolted out of the car and up to the dogs, who at that point appeared to be slightly tired out, but very pleased to see me with their tails wagging and the same "Did we do good?" smiles about them.

J.R. said: "I didn't know you were into sled dogs. Do you need some help getting them back?"

Now you'd think I'd have learned by that time, but pride combined with embarrassment makes a man do some real stupid things. "Nah," I said matter-of-factly. "This happens all the time. The little rascals have quite a bit of pep early in the year, but they'll settle down."

"It must get expensive running sleds on their sides like that," he said seriously, and I realized just then that the lashings on the right side of the sled were worn off as well as all of the finish. "You sure you don't want me to stay until your wife comes?"

"Nah, thanks anyway," I replied. "I'll just run them down the shoulder, nice and easy back home, you know, use the brake a lot." I actually figured that the dogs would stay tired. I also remembered the sled has a foot brake just below the driving bow, a good thing to know you have going down a hill. Besides, what else could go wrong? And so, J.R. left, and I followed.

I discovered four other things about mushing that morning: 1) A team of young huskies does not tire easily after a quick little five-mile jaunt, particularly when they are pulling an empty sled; 2) You don't really steer a dog sled; 3) Untrained dogs will run on the path of least resistance, which in this case was right down the center line of U.S. Highway 11; and 4) A conventional brake on a sled is virtually worthless on a snow-glazed highway.

The dogs bolted out of the ditch like the the hounds of hell. Then, after noticing that their sled was heavier than on their first cruise, they settled into a nice little 15-mph pace on the center line of the highway. I wasn't about to lose them or fall off again, and my time was occupied trying first to steer the sled onto the shoulder, then to call the dogs over to the shoulder (I guess I figured they instinctively knew what "Gee over" meant), then futilely trying to stop the sled.

Fortunately, there was virtually no one driving around that morning; and so after a few minutes, my confidence came back and I began to enjoy the ride. That was short-lived.

When we rounded the curve with Gold Shores Road (my corner) only about a third of a mile away, a pickup crested the top of the hill and was bearing down on us at highway speed.

I tried everything I could think of to steer the dogs or stop them or even slow them, but they just kept trotting along as if I wasn't there, oblivious to my maniacal ravings, happy as could be.

I knew I had to act quickly or we would all be killed. I climbed over the back of the sled, and then balanced my way to the front. I grabbed the bridle, then pulled myself onto to the back of the surprised wheel dogs, just in front of the sled. And then, no shit, I jumped from the wheel dogs to the point dogs and from the point dogs to the leaders, just like Dustin Hoffman did in the movie, *Little Big Man*, only he was doing it on a runaway horse wagon or something like that.

I grabbed the leaders' harnesses and reared back with all my might. Believe it or not, the dogs stopped dead in their tracks. When I looked up, the pickup was doing a series of donuts all over the slick road, 50 yards or so ahead of me. It also skidded to a stop in the middle of the highway with the driver's door about 10 feet from my leaders' noses. The window rolled down, and the red-faced owner, using language appropriate to the situation, suggested that I keep my dogs under control and off the highway. The only thing I could come up with to say was: "Why don't you keep your car under control. My dogs aren't doing donuts on this highway," which, of course, must have sounded goofy in retrospect.

In any event, the truck got going again, and so did we—just in time for my concerned wife and snickering children to find me and lead me back home. The rest of the trip was uneventful, and really so was the rest of the winter, because I didn't take out any more than three dogs until I had considerably more experience. I've since then had some other interesting experiences with my dog teams, but none quite as memorable as that first Halloween run in 1991.

Just for the Halibut

By: Buck Tilton

Rain falls with more predictability than sunshine in Sitka, the heart of southeast Alaska, but on this sea kayaking trip south of town, Jim and I had been surprised. Several dry hours had blessed three days of paddling. Still, I wore waterproof overalls that rose to my armpits and rubber boots. Across Sitka Sound, famous for its abundance of sealife, Mount Edgecumbe was an etching through thin morning clouds. Of Edgecumbe and rain, the native Tlingits say this: When you can't see the mountain, it's raining—when you can see it, it will rain soon.

But we floated lazily now in broken sunlight, Jim's red Folbot about 50 yards from my blue Klepper, jigging along the bottom for anything fishy for lunch, or dinner, depending on the fins of fortune. Hemlock and spruce crowd southeast Alaska's shoreline, and our camp was a dot of yellow nylon among the green, visible without eyestrain. Shoreline would be a pleasant and attractive memory soon.

Up until this moment, nothing in my life would have made Izaak Walton especially proud. Izaak said, "No man is born an angler." This morning, in fact, I'd hauled up a red starfish as big and appetizing as a garbage can lid, and an abandoned long line dangling several partially disintegrated hooks. Jim had boated a "snackerel," a small red snapper ... not even enough to fight over at feasting time. When the drift of the kayak stopped and my rod bent, I tugged and decided immediately I'd barbed a piece of submerged real estate. In 200 feet of saltwater, there's nothing to do but pull until something gives. What gave was the bottom. It started to rise slowly, with great effort by me, toward the surface. Jim paddled over to watch his idea of fun.

"Maybe you got the anchor off the boat that lost that long line," he offered helpfully. It felt that way.

Straining to lift, followed by spurts of frantic reeling, my eyes were on Jim's face when his color ran out like juice from a squeezed tomato and his eyes widened across his forehead. I glanced down to see a flash of white bigger than Denali. I must have asked, "What is it?" because I heard Jim mumble, "Dunno, dunno."

Another tug (what else could I do?) and a toilet bowl-sized mouth overflowing with long needles of teeth gaped into the light, followed by a crystal ball of an eye in which the future looked rather bleak. "Halibut!" screamed Jim, and simultaneously the fish determined she'd had enough. A surge of power awesomely indescribable to someone not hooked to it, and the fish exploded out of watery starting blocks with me surfing behind and grateful the Klepper's foot-operated rudder allowed me to follow instead of being flipped. Only a miracle explains why the 50-pound test line didn't break then, or later.

I heard another yell from Jim, "Don't let go!" Let go? I'd laid out close to $200 for this here stout rod and the heavy Penn reel.

Suddenly my mind slowed. Images of recent events flowed like mercury in a frigid thermometer. Old Nels waving us off with the hand he only had part of. "Halibut bit it off," he explained in a gruff Norwegian accent. The recent newspaper story of the lone fisherman who hauled a huge halibut over the gunwale of his small Boston Whaler to have it beat him to death.

The world's largest flat fish, *Hippoglossus vulgaris* (such an appropriate name!), hatches looking pretty much like any old fish, but then something goes wrong. One eye migrates to the same side of the head as the other eye, and they spend the rest of their lives lying and swimming with the no-eye-side down. The downside turns white and the upside brown. I figure looking weird and never getting to see what's underneath before they lie down has given every halibut a real bad disposition. With huge mouths and ravenous appetites, they've been measured at more than 10 feet in length and 585 pounds in weight ... most of it is muscle. That's a heck of a lot of meanness.

We were headed—this psychologically unstable fish and I—gracefully for Japan ... or maybe Siberia. By the time I was calm enough to peek over my shoulder, land was extinct and Jim was a red slash paddling furiously but unable to keep up. All calmness fled. Cut the line! my brain suggested to my trembling hands. Cut the line! Although we were much closer to Asia than we were to Colorado, I don't speak Japanese ... or Russian. And I had failed to pack a lunch.

Pinning the rod with my knees and one hand, I dug a jackknife out of the chest pocket of my overalls and was trying to open it with my canines, when the halibut began a long sweeping turn that ended with the kayak pointed back toward Jim. I passed him with what I hoped was a shrug of casual fatalism. "Don't let go," he reminded me.

Halibut and I overtook and passed two low-flying bald eagles and a large diesel-powered professional fisherman before the fish wore out and dropped to rest on a stretch of sandy bottom, about 30 yards from shore. Not much water separated us. I could see her below, carpeting the seafloor.

Jim paddled up sweaty and flushed. It was good to see his color returned. What now? We debated in hushed whispers and decided to paddle to shore and try to beach her.

Clamping the rod between my thighs and letting out line, I eased to land and stepped out on shaky legs. Working together, Jim and I leaned into the rod and felt the fish move just a little. Inch by inch, we encouraged her closer and closer to shore, telling ourselves the

line would snap with the next pull so we wouldn't be so disappoint-
ed when it did, until she would move no more. Jim walked to the
water's edge, and said she was close, real close. "Go get it," I said.
"Go to hell," he responded.

Sitting down with the rod cradled in limp arms, I waited for two
hours meditating on the words of Samuel Johnson who said fishing
was "a worm at one end and a fool at the other." The tide went out
and left the halibut high and somewhat dry. She never budged as the
water receded down her considerable length. When it appeared safe,
Jim hefted a weighty rock, of which most of Alaska's coast is made,
and dropped it thunderously on the fish's head. Her budgelessness
ended abruptly and the line snapped. Freed, freed at last from the
tether that had bound me for more than four hours. Giggling with
mild hysteria, I walked light-headed to where the fish had wildly
flopped her last flop, above the cold sea wave's reach.

Tying her with quarter-inch nylon cord to drag beneath both our
sterns, she tipped our combined bows toward the sky as we paddled
back to camp. Curiosity brought the big diesel fisherman alongside,
and he hoisted her on his scale where she hung at 240 pounds. "A
female, and a giant," he said, then he grumbled something colorful
about "outsiders." Being a man who earned his living from what he
drug aboard, the act of lowering the halibut back down to us was
performed with blatant reluctance. I tried to assume my oh-just-
another-day-of-fishing-from-a-70-pound-boat expression.

Before we reached our campsite, I noticed I was drenched, and
rain was pattering down with temperate maritime persistence. Mount
Edgecumbe, sure enough, was invisible. I grinned over at Jim as
stupidly as I thought he was grinning at me. "A fool," wrote
Napoleon, "has one great advantage over a man of sense—he is
always satisfied with himself."

The Malay Melee

By: Mark Deem

In Jarantut, Malaysia, at 4:30 a.m., there's no place to get coffee. Dave and I had stumbled off the train from Singapore into the middle of the Malaysian Muslim equivalent of an Old West town. Sitting on our backpacks, huddled in a doorway against the rain, rumpled and half asleep, we wondered about the penalties for vagrancy in a land where stealing an orange could earn you the nickname, "Lefty."

The train ride from Singapore had been hell. I had spent hours laying awake in a top sleeping berth on the Malay railroad, watching blue sparks fly from the back of an ancient fan bolted to the ceiling. Finally hypnotized into a fitful sleep, I awoke with a start to the popping sound of the fan shorting out. Dave was sound asleep in the lower berth, but I spent the next two hours sweating upstairs, choking on the smoke from a Malay couple across the aisle. Both their cigarettes and their babbling seemed endless. I had no idea what they were smoking, but the stench of it would have made the Marlboro Man retch.

We were on our way to Taman Negara, one of the largest national parks in Southeast Asia. The guidebook told of virgin rain forest, wondrous animal life and a two-hour boat ride upriver just to reach park headquarters. From there, we backpacked to "hides," cabins on

stilts overlooking mineral licks. From the hides, if you were very quiet and a little lucky, you could observe the jungle denizens.

The town finally woke up, and 6 a.m. found us fed, filled with coffee and on the wrong bus to the boat dock. In Southeast Asia, you quickly learn that there are two buses involved in any trip—the first one you get on and the right one, which an angry ticket taker usually shoves you onto once he or she figures out where you're really going.

It took us another two and a half hours to reach the park headquarters, wedged between fuel drums and cases of Nescafe, in a glorified rowboat with a car engine strapped to the back. River otters and kingfishers dove into the river, swollen by the first rains of the monsoon season.

After checking in, we took off through the bush. At first the trail followed the river, and we skidded up and down steep, mud-slicked banks into the many tributaries emptying into the Tembeling River. After a couple of attempted crossings, we gave up on staying dry, and simply heaved our packs on top of our heads and trudged through the rivers in our boots. The air was so hot and thick with moisture, it was impossible to tell if the liquid streaming down our shirts and rippling off our chests was sweat or water from the latest crossing.

After a few miles, the track turned inland, and we were glad to leave the slip-and-splash river crossings. Our joy quickly faded as we began to notice the rain forest's most prolific creatures—leeches. After a mile or so on the inland trail, mucking through ankle-deep mud and standing water, Dave looked down to find a legion of the little bloodsuckers trying to find their way into his socks. We developed a routine of swapping leads every mile or so. The man in front was "Spiderman," taking all of the spiderwebs which draped the little used trail on the chin. The second was the "Leech Zambony," the guy the leeches latched onto after being awakened by the vibration of Spiderman's passing.

We finally reached the hide, exhausted and dehydrated from the lack of water stops during our inland hike. It felt strange to be dehydrated in the rain forest during monsoon season, but the leeches had relentlessly driven us on. Every time we had tried to stop for water, a circle of the little vampires would advance on us.

Sucking on saltines and peanut butter, I peeled off my sodden T-shirt, wrung a 3-foot-wide puddle of sweat out of it, then set up camp. We took turns with our flashlights scanning the mineral licks for wildlife. After a few hours of this, our flashlights and our faculties dimming, we turned in. The disappointment of not spotting any animals dimmed as the symphony of the forest kicked into a frenzied overture. Species of insects and birds, so numerous they had all yet to be named, weaved their calls into a fabric of sound that would have made Mozart shred his sheet music and take up hockey. A sudden crash of thunder cut through the crescendo. A solid wall of water fell from the sky, meeting a solid canopy of leaves with a slap. Dave and I drifted off to sleep as the rain forest earned its name.

Sometime during the night, I awoke to a loud shuffling sound. As my waking disorientation wore off, I realized that it wasn't Dave heading out to answer the call of nature. It was a definite stop-and-start shuffling, coming from somewhere between Dave's bunk and mine. From the top bunk across the hide from me, I could hear Dave trying to quietly locate his flashlight. We both switched our beams on and shined them at each other.

"Rat?" Dave mouthed silently. Jungle rats, big furry foot-long monsters in search of leftover tourist food, were regular visitors to the hides. I shrugged, and Dave and I dimmed the beams with our hands and slowly searched the floor. It took several cycles of shuffle, silence, searchlight before our crisscrossing beams met simultaneously at the source of the noise.

A spider. Not just your run-of-the-mill movie tarantula-type spider. This thing was the god of all nightmares, frozen in our flashlight beams in the middle of the jungle, in the middle of the night, in the middle of a crashing monsoon rain. Its body alone was the size of a dinner plate, and its long black legs were hairy enough to make a Berkeley girl want to shave.

We each raised our beams up to look at the other. I imagined Dave's wide-eyed, shocked, nervous face as an exact mirror of my own. His expression said, "Now what?" I shrugged, wishing that we had opted to carry our mosquito net tubes on this hike. The shuffling resumed, and we snapped our beams back onto our new roommate, who was making for the corner. He froze when our lights found him, and the three of us remained at a standstill for several minutes.

I sat there considering our options. Kill it? I didn't want to hurt it, and besides, the biggest thing we had around was a hiking boot, which it probably could have worn comfortably, and which also was about a foot away from the beast. Throw it out of the hide? I was pretty sure it would be able to take me two out of three falls. Hike back to headquarters? Yeah, right—dark ... rain ... leeches ... rivers—not an option. As I was thinking, Dave shut off his light and curled up on his bunk. I shined my beam back and forth between him and the spider several times before doing the same. In the absolute dark that followed, our new friend shuffled around the hide while I tried not to think about webs and flies. The sound of his wanderings gradually blended into the hiss of the jungle rain, and I slipped into a very light sleep.

From Rookie to Expert

By: Anthony Richards

In the summer of my 19th year, I was working as a mountain climbing instructor and was assigned to my first European destination in Saas Fee, Switzerland. Prior to the first clients arriving from England, I had to prepare for the routes and mountains we were to climb. As with most Alpine ascents, it is necessary to climb to a mountain hut at about 6,000 feet on the first day. This is done in order to make an early predawn start the next day so that climbing up and down from the summit is completed before the afternoon sun softens the snow and creates an avalanche threat.

I was staying at one of these huts for a few days to explore the various routes and become acclimatized. The hut was situated above the tree line. It was nestled on the side of the mountain overlooking the glacier below. There were several top European mountaineers residing here, and I was viewed as the rookie hot shot from England who was brought up on the gritstone crags of Derbyshire and the dark cliffs of North Wales. They were anxious to see how I would fare in their high alps with the ice and rarified air.

These mountain huts are somewhat spartan with large communal beds and centralized kitchens. The bathroom facilities were confined to an outhouse which was precariously perched on the side of the mountain. Whereas I was not unfamiliar with this style of living and the use of outhouses, this particular one proved to be quite unique. It was a two-holer by design and was built on a platform that overhung the glacier. Even though the structure was secured to the mountainside with sturdy cables, the wind had a tendency to take charge and shake the structure at will.

When in a new culture, I have learned to hang back and observe before rushing in. This was no exception, despite my sense of urgency to use the facility. Sitting on a rock outside the hut, I watched an "expert" mountaineer take the narrow trail to the outhouse. On his way, he stopped to collect small rocks about the size of large mothballs. He loaded these into his pocket and proceeded to use the outhouse. After some time, he returned to the main hut and it was my turn.

Dutifully I followed the ritual of the "expert" and loaded my pockets with about a dozen rocks. Upon entering the outhouse, I was amazed at the noise created by the wind rushing up through the hole in the floor. As I peered down the hole, I could see the glacier some several hundred feet below. The wind was not warm and together with the swaying of the platform, I cut my activity as short as possible. The toilet paper was hanging on the wall out of reach. However, when I had finished with the paper, I found that it was impossible to dispose of it down the hole because of the wind coming up. In fact, my first attempt adhered to the ceiling!

Being a quick-thinking fellow, I remembered my pocketful of rocks. It then became obvious. The second attempt at disposing of the paper was successful when wrapped around the rocks. There was intense satisfaction in hurling these missiles against the elements to the glacier below.

I am not sure how environmentally friendly this form of sanitation might be. However, I quickly changed my diet so that my visits became less frequent. With this sense of mastery and increased self-esteem, you can imagine the pleasure I had teaching this particular skill to my clients who were generally used to modern plumbing with gold fittings. To this day, I do not venture into the outdoors without at least a few pebbles in my pocket. After all, I am now an "expert."

Nature Woman Meets Lightning

By: Lorrie Parker

I started getting a queasy feeling in my stomach as my new
boyfriend, John, and I drove through the gates of the "Saddle de
Sade" Ranch. Not only had I twisted the facts a little about my
riding ability; but the place itself seemed strange to me. The moun-
tains and fields before me were beautiful, but it seemed odd that all
the horses were black.

John glanced over and caught me fidgeting. "You're not afraid,
are you? Your personal ad had you listed as a nature woman who
loves to have outdoor adventures."

"Oh no, of course not. I was just trying to remember whether
or not I watered my coonhounds before I left. I'm an avid hunter,
you know." I felt I had to lie. It's so hard to find a good, honest
man anymore.

John reached over and patted my knee. I adjusted my cute little
cowgirl hat and smiled my brightest fake smile.

We pulled up in front of the stables, and out stepped a scary looking woman dressed in black leather. She stroked her braided black whip as she smiled (which looked more like a smirk to me) and said: "Welcome to the 'Saddle de Sade.' Sign these release forms, fork over the $10 each, and we'll be off on our little ride."

"Do we get to pick out our own horse?" I managed to ask, despite the frog in my throat.

"I will assign the horses to you," she said, as she fondled the spurs attached to her black boots. I'm sure I heard her chuckling as she turned away.

John got Lucifer. I got Lightning.

Lucifer was a sleek black, prancing steed. Lightning was a dull black, clunky type, who looked as though he might have had a moose for a grandfather on one side or the other.

I was disappointed with Lightning's appearance, but I was happy to note that he didn't look too fast or dangerous (as his name implied). We climbed aboard our mounts, and the trail mistress led us off. Well, she led John off. Lightning must have eaten a trough full of prunes before he left his stall, so he stood there happily fertilizing the earth beneath me. When he finally squeezed the last one out, I kicked and clucked and jerked around on his back in my Daisy Duke shorts until he plodded off after the other horses, who were, by now, almost out of sight.

We made it about 20 feet, then Lightning spotted a clump of sorry-looking grass that he just had to devour. Another few feet away, he stretched his thick neck to the limit to nip off all the leaves within his reach.

Suddenly, I saw the trail mistress turn her horse and come galloping back toward me. She circled her stallion to come up behind my unsuspecting tree-munching lump, and gave him a wicked crack on his substantial rump with her whip. Lightning lurched forward, causing my new hat to fly off and land in one of his many contributions to the land. He continued on for about five minutes in a clumsy trot that made me wish I'd padded my new Daisy Duke shorts.

Then he saw some more grass he couldn't pass up, then more leaves. Then he had to poop again, and again, until the wicked trail mistress came charging back to repeat her act with the whip.

John looked back occasionally, waving and shouting words I couldn't hear over Lightning's chomping and expelling. I smiled and waved back as I thought of the future dates we'd have that wouldn't be outdoors.

I consoled myself with the thought that I hadn't made a fool of myself by chickening out at the last minute, or falling off my horse. I was actually beginning to enjoy the scenery around me, until we rounded that last bend of the ride.

Lightning saw the stables, and his peanut-sized brain remembered that the stables held food. He tossed his huge head, reared up and proceeded to show me how he had earned his name.

He galloped past John and the trail mistress as fast as a bat, while I tried like hell to hold on. He didn't stop until he slid to a halt in front of his pile of hay (and prunes) in the stable.

Luckily, I had enough time to fall out of the saddle, brush my windblown hair, wipe my teary eyes and dry my wet Daisy Dukes with an old saddle blanket, before John and the smirking trail mistress rode in.

John's eyes were shining as he dismounted and walked toward me.

"You really are an adventurer!" he exclaimed. "I can't wait until our next date. I'll take you hang gliding."

I hobbled toward the car on my newly bowed legs. "I'm sorry, John, but I'm busy that day. I have to bathe my coonhounds. We're going to go snipe hunting."

One Nasty Ice Capade

By: Paul Suwalski

I met Howard while working a five-month contract in Antarctica. Howard was a middle-aged electrician from Florida; he hated the cold, but the money was good and he was in need of the character building that the Antarctic provided. Florida had made him soft. Actually, it was very normal to hate the Antarctic shortly after landing on the frozen Ross Sea. We all dispassionately referred to this lost landscape as "the ice."

Chuck was the finest snowmobile mechanic on the continent. The Antarctic had only three such mechanics, if you count the French, who had a vile encampment nearby. Anyway, Chuck owed me a great favor. I talked him out of a broken leg. However, I got the better end of the deal, since Chuck would later save my life.

One particularly nasty morning, Chuck was begging me to back over his leg with the six-ton dump truck that I was driving. He was hoping for an air medi-vac to New Zealand where life was much nicer. He was mumbling something about women, fried chicken and sheep. I jumped out of my truck and with the compassion of Rush

Limbaugh, consoled Chuck. This was not easy, since he was groveling on the dirty snow. He then began uttering what sounded like territorial seal noises and began grinding his teeth incessantly. This distressed me deeply, and annoyed the neighboring harem of leopard seals. I explained to him that things were not as bad as they appeared. This was a tough sell. Chuck was overweight, underemployed and had a confirmed drinking problem. Oddly enough, I was underweight, over employed and had an unconfirmed drinking problem. It's scary, but a weird polarity exists near the South Pole.

It appeared "the ice" was getting the best of Chuck. Could it be the lack of decent food, real sex and subzero temperatures was causing his dementia? The continuous daylight could also make one nuts. Hey, I'm no psychologist, but I knew Chuck needed an empathetic ear.

I carefully listened to Chuck's complaints, and replied that both sex and fried chicken were vastly overrated. I also explained that the sheer weight of my truck would squash his leg like an overcooked zucchini, and that New Zealand was a good 18 years behind the art of fitting prostheses. Chuck got up off the ground wiping the frozen snot from his beard. I told him that in just two months he'd be back in Denver as a fleet mechanic for a rental car company. He'd be watching reruns of the Broncos that his ex-girlfriend recorded on the VCR she never returned. Bad move. Chuck returned to grinding his teeth, snorting and making other rude noises. He then placed his stubby leg back under the rear dual tires of my dump truck. I never should have mentioned the Broncos or his VCR.

I was desperate. I told him that his job was important, and I'd buy the drinks after work. I also mentioned a little ditty I learned in Catholic school: "Today, my friend, is the first day of the rest of your life!" It worked as if divine intervention entered his modest brain—not to mention the fact that my watch alarm sounded for our 10 a.m. coffee break.

Chuck made a dramatic 180-degree turn in his attitude and during the subsequent days actually seemed happy. This made me ponder if I should stop driving this dump truck in the awful Antarctic and become an evangelist on a Caribbean cruise line.

A week passed. I ran into Chuck at his snowmobile shop. He asked me if I'd like to join him after work to visit Howard, who was about to endure his first night of survival school.

This would be fun. Howard hated the cold. Howard would hate survival school. Best of all, he was required to participate! Chuck and I would enjoy agitating Howard as he dug his cave, the one he would have to spend the night in. There was also a good chance that Howard might freeze to death, since he was a warm-blooded native of Cocoa Beach. I suggested we bring our cameras. I was also glad that despite Chuck's recent bout of serenity, he still had come malice festering inside.

After our work day ended, Chuck and I sucked down a bottle of amaretto. This was Chuck's favorite, and it nicely warmed our insides. We saddled our snowmobiles and headed in the general direction of the survival school. We had skipped dinner and we were drunk as pigs. It was about 9 p.m. and the ever-present and maddening sun was shining brightly. Fearlessly, we roared through the formidable landscape. We were on a mission to make sure Howard was miserable during his last few conscious moments. In fact, these would be Kodak moments, since I brought along my trusty camera.

Chuck said he knew a shortcut and barked, "Follow me!" He unknowingly led us through a deadly crevasse field. We'd been riding for some time and my amaretto laced stomach was toasty, just the rest of me was cold. In fact, I detected my balls ascending into some uncharted region near my duodenum. I also found I couldn't talk very well, or blink very well for that matter since my eyeballs were frozen in an open position. Still, I faithfully followed Chuck's deep snowmobile tracks.

Suddenly, without any warning, my world turned white. I dropped. Propelled forward, I conked my head on the Plexiglas windshield. It was as if someone pulled out the white carpet I had been riding on so confidently. I realized I had broken through a snow bridge and was precariously lodged in a crevasse. I sobered up quickly. My snowmobile was slipping into its icy grave. I assessed my grim situation. I had to get my chewy butt out of there. I stood atop the seat, jumped onto the lip of the crevasse and pulled myself to safety. It was a slick maneuver. Very macho.

Chuck was oblivious to my predicament, and I saw his orange snowmobile fade into the white void. Oh shit! I may die stranded. Ten minutes passed, but they felt like two hours. Finally, I saw Chuck heading back to my rescue! As he pulled up I saw a look of drunken consternation, not unlike what I imagine Ted Kennedy looked like at Chappaquiddick. An amber spittle encrusted his beard—frozen amaretto. He was obviously pissed and growled: "Nice going, numbnuts. I'm responsible for these snowmobiles!"

I retorted, "I'm sorry, redbeard, but where the hell are you taking us, the freakin' Bermuda Triangle?"

Unfettered, he responded: "We've got to get this rig out. You could get fired!" Terrific. I pondered if that would include my end-of-season bonus. Chuck then took a cable from his snowmobile, carefully descended into the crevasse and attached the cord around my dead sled. Chuck then ran the cable to his rig and proceeded to try and pull the sucker out.

Chuck throttled and redlined his snowmobile to no avail. The two-cycle noxious exhaust blew in my face. I walked backward to avoid the fumes and dropped through another snow bridge! Luckily, my arms caught the edge of the crevasse and I held on for dear life. I looked over my shoulder and saw the icy blue water a good 30 feet below. Oh shit, again! My sphincter involuntarily slammed shut like a bathtub drain, making a dull thud rather like a dead trout hitting an Italian marble floor. This was awful.

Chuck couldn't hear my frantic screams, since his engine was winding out 20 feet away. My goose down parka slipped against my modest hold. The snow crumbled out from under my arms, and I continually lunged along the crevasse lip for a secure position. This was not fun. I hung, and hung ... and then accepted my imminent death. Will I drown in the freezing water below, or will I manage to stay afloat and die of hypothermia? Ultimately, I will become food for the sea urchins. Sadly enough, I probably deserved such a dismal fate. Still, I hung on and my arms began to burn like you wouldn't believe.

Next, a strange thing happened. I say a chronological flashback of the significant moments from my life. I saw my kindergarten teacher, with liver spots and blue hair; the mean nuns that tortured me daily and taught me guilt. I relived the sheer ecstasy of receiving my driver's license, selling my first magazine article, and the steamy hot tub incident with Jane. The sad moments replayed also in painful detail: dropping a good bottle of scotch and my Dad's funeral. Howard also owed me 20 bucks. I must live ... and collect! Howard must live! Twenty bucks!

Chuck seized the engine of his snowmobile, and cussed like a sailor. I mustered a scream, and Chuck finally saw me clinging for my life. He ran and grabbed me by my armpits, and pulled me onto terra firma. Exhausted and in a pathetic fetal position, I contemplated kissing Chuck's filthy snow boots. I asked for a drink instead.

Chuck and I rode tandem back to town. We were both quiet. My snowmobile was left in the crevasse with my camera. My brush with death made me feel unusually aware of the surroundings. A surreal beauty became apparent. I also felt damn lucky. Two co-workers died in a nearby crevasse a month earlier. They took a fatal shortcut while on a hike.

Almost a decade has passed. I have quit drinking and working on the ice. I've lost contact with Chuck but remain eternally grateful to him for saving my life. Howard survived his night in the snow cave and settled in sunny Florida. Funny, I never did get my 20 bucks. Thanks Chuck. Life is good.

Northern Exposure

By: David Scott

Alone we stood on the brink of a great adventure. The nearest town (Churchill) was 120 miles northeast from where we stood, and in some directions the nearest human being was a thousand miles away. We stood among 2,000 pounds of food and provisions stuffed into labeled duffel bags. Around us lay a pristine wilderness devoid of human footprints. Ahead of us was one year of hardships, darkness, danger and adventure in a land as beautiful as it was deadly.

My partner, Scott Power, and I were embarking on the trip that had only been a dream for years. Spending one full year in a remote wilderness cabin, miles from "modern conveniences," in the northeastern corner of Manitoba, Canada.

Dr. William Forgey built the cabin in the summer of '76; and after meeting him in 1989, I had heard nothing but white knuckle stories of "The North."

Now, however, the dream was as real as the cold that sank its icy teeth into my skin. Did I forget to mention that we were beginning our trip in late January? Earlier that morning, Hap, our bush pilot, said we would have to wait until the temperature "warmed up" to 40 below zero before he could safely fly. All we had to do was hike

from where we were (Landing Lake) to the cabin, a simple three-mile jaunt, or so we thought.

Scott, who was 20 at the time, and I, 19, approached this adventure with great confidence, yet the wilderness, as always, was quick to change all that.

It was 2 o'clock in the afternoon, and already the sunlight was fading. We strapped on our snowshoes hastily, eager to start hiking, eager to become warm. Scott retrieved the map from his pack and we aimed our compasses toward our destination. We each shouldered our packs and began the journey.

After 10 steps, I knew this was going to be a grueling hike. The trees locked limbs making travel difficult and navigation nearly impossible. Because of the intense cold, the snow was like powdered sugar. Instead of walking upon it, we punched through it, carrying the weight of the snow that piled on our snowshoes with every step. We figured the hike would take us no more than three hours, four at the very most. Three hours later we were still hiking, and we couldn't even see the river valley. We were growing tired, thirsty and hungry. Our water was gone and our energy bars quickly became unappealing. Yet, onward we trudged, pacing ourselves and pausing every hundred steps to catch our breath, still quite content, still quite naive.

After four hours, Scott grabbed my arm, "There it is," he said. "The river." I squinted only to see the silvery vein of the Little Beaver River shining like a neon ribbon in the pale light of a full moon. With newfound energy, we began hiking down the gradual slope when I remembered what Dr. Forgey had once told me.

"When you can see the river, you're halfway there."

Halfway there, I thought. Well, Doc always did have a way of exaggerating, we're surely more than halfway there. Yet we continued to hike, the temperature continued to drop, and our eagerness continued to grow. Four hours later, we stepped from the trees and onto the frozen river. Little did we know that 200 miles south of us in Thompson the temperature hovered at 60 below zero.

Scott had been to the cabin once before in 1989. I turned to him and asked with a pathetic ring of hope in my voice, "Is this it? Is this the right place?"

"Well, the cabin is on a wide bend in the river," he said. "This certainly looks like the place, it should be right over there."

He pointed to a spot on the river bank 100 yards away. The cold was overpowering, an invisible killer from which we could not hide. Our bodies were dehydrated and craving fuel, but home was only a few steps away.

We walked in the direction that Scott pointed, but when we got there we saw only the same dense forest that we'd been hiking through.

"Maybe it's farther upstream," Scott suggested.

We walked upstream, then downstream, zigzagging in and out of the trees on the bank with no luck. For two hours, we searched for the cabin we had flown over only 12 hours earlier, but found nothing.

Our situation was now desperate. I made the foolish mistake of assuming that we should not carry the extra weight of a tent, assuming we would find the cabin. Such a mistake paralleled climbing Mount Everest and assuming a rope is unnecessary.

Scott howled a curse into the star-filled sky, but the wind simply sighed, knocking several puffs of snow from their tree-limb perches silently to the forest floor.

We had to build a shelter, and we had to build one fast. We needed warmth, for ours was slowly slipping away. A snow cave would have been ideal, but the snow would not pack, which left us with building an A-frame from pine boughs.

Scott and I worked vigorously, and in half an hour we had our shelter, or perhaps our grave. Inside, we laid more pine boughs, followed by our sleeping pads for added insulation. On the sleeping pads, we spread an open sleeping bag, followed by another bag which both Scott and I climbed into. Once in the bag, we pulled the open bag around us and hugged to share what little heat we had. Finally, we prepared ourselves for the longest, the coldest and perhaps the final night of our lives.

Sleep came in half-hour intervals, and each time one of us would wake up, we would ask the other, "You OK?" The response generally was stuttered from the cold, "Y ... y ... yeah, I'm OK."

So it went for the next six hours. This was the odyssey of the North, this was the fate bestowed upon us, and this was only the beginning of a dream turned nightmare. I thought of the creatures around us who needed nothing but instincts to survive. How foolish I was to approach this land with such confidence. How foolish I was to be anything but humble. Even with everything, how envious I was of the animals who had nothing. I reflected on something Doc had once told me, "You know you're in a wilderness, when you can yell your head off for help, and no one will hear you." I knew at last I was in such a place.

Throughout the night, I kept believing someone would come and save us, but back home our friends and family felt confident Scott and I were slugging back mugs of hot chocolate in front of the wood-burning stove. If they only knew.

I woke up the following morning and peered through the lacelike branches of our poorly made shelter. Although the sun was shining it was dreadfully cold. The night had taken its toll for my body was stiff with pain, yet on the positive side, we were alive.

I climbed from the bag and struggled to get into my frozen mukluks. Again, Scott and I searched the bank of the river; and again, we found no cabin.

We hadn't eaten a solid meal in 20 hours, and it had been nearly that long since our last decent drink. We decided to travel back to Landing Lake and set up one of the tents stowed there.

The trip went quickly since we had already made a snowshoe trail the day before. Three hours later, we were setting up our faithful Eureka Drawtight, a canvas expedition tent that, when used in conjunction with a kerosene stove, is a virtual mobile home.

Of course, there remained a slight problem. The elbow section of the stovepipe was at the cabin. We knew this before embarking on the trip, yet who would have thought we'd use this tent before using the cabin?

Fortunately, we had some aluminum foil in one of the duffel bags, so we figured we could rig something, not the safest idea in the world, but we were in a bit of a pinch.

I filled the stove with fuel while Scott prepared the stovepipe; and in no time, the tiny stove was lit. The inside of our tent slowly became warm and I gathered snow to melt for water. At last, we were displaying a bit of control over our situation.

The pot of snow on the stove was slowly turning into a liquid form, when Scott suddenly claimed to smell smoke. Soon I too smelled the strong odor of kerosene; and upon looking up, I discovered the top of our tent near the door was in flames. I grabbed the pot of water a split second before Scott swatted the stove out the door and into the snow. With our big down mitts, Scott and I began slapping out the flames, shouting curses as we worked.

The task took no more than a minute to complete, yet when I looked down, I saw what was once the only form of liquid for 200 miles was now frozen solid.

Outside, the stove sat hissing in a ring of melted snow. Neither Scott nor I said a word, we simply climbed into our sleeping bags, while the evening sky peered at us through a huge black eye in the roof of our tent.

During the night, we were hit by a typical northern storm that forced us to climb out of our bags and hold the inside walls of the tent to keep them from collapsing.

I contemplated this chain of events, I thought about Murphy's Law and I attempted to figure out where the cabin was that we had flown over two days earlier. We had meticulously planned for months in advance. Each detail, from every penny to every pound, was looked at with careful consideration.

The following morning was as unpleasant as the previous morning. Breakfast consisted of frozen granola bars and mouthfuls of snow. We decided to head back to the river, this time with a more modern geodesic dome tent and a small, one-burner, white gas stove.

Again the trip was completed quickly. Our only source of energy was the anger built up from the past two days. I knew our azimuth was correct, but I could not figure out why we were not at the cabin.

By the time we reached the river, we were exhausted, but without hesitation, Scott and I began setting up the tent. Again another problem remained.

The shock cords that ran through the aluminum tent poles when pulled apart would not contract, so we had to cut all of the cords from the poles. This sounds easy enough, but at 40 below, it was an arduous task. We had to watch our fingers in order to accomplish such a job, for the cold prevented anything from being done merely by touch. Under normal circumstances, our tent took less than three minutes to erect, now it took more than a half an hour.

Hypothermia was making its presence known. Movements were lethargic, speech was slurred and the shivering that was once overpowering was now fading away.

Scott and I climbed into the tent and dug out the small one-burner stove. In such cold temperatures, the stove would not function without first being primed. I poured a small portion of white gas into the burner on the stove and touched it with a match, which caused it to ignite with an audible "poof." We were instantly wrapped within the arms of warmth.

Our first job was food and water. Scott opened the tent door, retrieved a pot full of fresh snow and placed it on the hissing stove. At last, we were finally beginning to display a bit of control over our situation. As long as our fuel held out, we would be safe.

That night, excitement filled the small dome tent. We felt confident that we would find the cabin in the morning, and we reviewed all of our maps in search of clues.

Finally, with bellies full of food and drink and bodies comfortably warm from the stove's heat, we crawled into our bags and shut down the stove. The night air was still and the temperature continued to drop.

"Tomorrow," I thought.

I did not wake up to the hollowed songs of wind blowing through the trees that morning, instead I heard the colorful array of curses Scott was whispering to himself.

"What's the matter?" I asked

Scott said nothing, he simply held his bare foot up in the air. It was as black as a northern winter night, frostbitten to the third degree.

"No shit," I said, too baffled to say anything else.

The silence was overpowering; and for the longest time, Scott and I simply stared at the peculiar color of his foot. Luckily, before we left for Canada, we had been through extensive medical training by Dr. Forgey.

"I'll head to Landing Lake and get the medical kit," I told Scott, knowing that he could not risk refreezing his foot.

I put on all of my winter gear, climbed out of the tent and began the hike to Landing Lake. I was disappointed that we could not look for the cabin, but safety came first.

I made the trip there and back as quickly as possible and found Scott lying in the tent with small pieces of cotton between his toes.

"I got the medical kit along with more fuel and a box of macaroni and cheese." I said with excitement hoping his spirits would cheer.

It was too late to immerse his foot in 110-degree water, so he simply bandaged the foot and took the proper antibiotics. The next morning I had to find the cabin, enough was enough.

Day 5, February 2. I was awake well before the sun, and from my bag, I watched the sky beyond the tent's ceiling turn from slate gray to pale blue.

I reached over and ignited the stove without leaving the confines of my warm bag. Coffee was, of course, the first thing on the menu, very strong, very black coffee.

Scott still slept soundly and I contemplated our predicament—more importantly, his predicament. The sight of his foot made me nervous. I knew, without the cabin, his condition would only become worse.

Once he was awake and we had breakfast, I donned my winter garb and bolted out to greet the frozen day. The sky was crisp and blue, and the land was as beautiful as ever.

I wasted no time strapping on my snowshoes; and as I turned to tackle the trail, Scott called out to me.

"Hey," I heard him say, despite the many layers of wool and down covering my ears, "be careful."

I headed upstream at a brisk pace peering into the southern banks like a starved predator hungry for anything that appeared man-made. I weaved in and out of the tree line threading a course with clumsy steps, but searching, always searching.

After a mile had fallen behind me, I found myself staring into the mouth of a feeder stream—a stream that Scott and I would later name Paradise Creek.

The trees that grew upon its banks were the largest I had seen which gave me a rather bizarre idea. I removed my snowshoes and proceeded to climb. I thought that with a bird's-eye-view I could see something that I was missing from the ground.

The limbs tore at my bare face, and I'm sure I appeared quite out of context to the unseen animals around me. With great patience, I reached the top, and although I did not see the cabin, I did see a clue that would perhaps take me to its front door.

What I saw was a lake, a very small lake, but one that could not be seen from the ground. If I could locate the same lake on the map I had a chance of discovering where we were in relation to the cabin.

I scampered down the tree nearly falling several times in my state of haste. The sun was beginning to set as I strapped on my snowshoes; and in no time, I was rounding the bend to our tiny dome tent.

As I drew nearer, I heard Scott's eager voice ask the inevitable, "Well ... did ya' find it?"

I unzipped the door and dove inside placing my hands over the warmth of the stove. Grabbing the map, I explained my theory, and after one glance, I hoped I was right.

Sleep did not come easily that night. The temperature dropped and the winds howled. How far away home seemed, how inaccessible. I tossed and turned wondering if our other home awaited one mile downstream. We had no choice but to bet our lives on it.

When Scott woke up the following morning, I was already cooking breakfast. As we ate, neither of us said a word about finding the cabin, we did not want to jinx ourselves.

Again, I ambled out of the tent and strapped on my snowshoes, and again, Scott told me to be careful. The jagged fangs of spruce trees stabbed into the sun on the eastern horizon, and before I could take 10 steps, Scott stopped me once more.

"Hey," he said, with his head sticking out of the tent, "good luck."

I gave him the thumbs-up sign and started walking. My snowshoes crunched through the powdery snow and it seemed as though I was walking on a treadmill.

Again my eyes panned the bank of the river. After rounding the first bend, the river was straight. I looked at the map and indeed the river was straight. Even the subtle topography seemed to match. Yet I didn't get my hopes up. I knew from the past six days how the mind can play tricks when desperate.

I continued to walk, staring into the trees, when I saw something that appeared out of the ordinary. For the past mile, the trees were a solid wall without so much as a single break. Yet, at this spot, I saw a break just large enough to be a trail. I took two more steps when, through the trees, I saw a large mound of snow.

I held my breath and began walking toward what I thought could very well be a cabin. My heart pounded and my legs suddenly felt heavy. The ever present sound of the wind was no longer there, and it seemed as if all that existed was myself and what I hoped was a cabin.

When I passed through the curtain of pine boughs, my efforts were rewarded. There before me, wrapped in a royal robe of white, sat the cabin. I fell to my knees and stared. The cold that was burning my flesh was replaced with a sudden rush of warmth.

After several minutes, I stood and walked closer to the structure. Never before had I seen anything so beautiful, so simple. I removed my down mitts and placed both hands on the cabin walls, indeed it was real.

I gave it a quick inspection to make certain everything was in working order; and although I did not want to leave, I could wait no longer to tell Scott the good news.

As I turned to hike down the path that lead to the river, I paused to look once more at the quiet cabin. I was no longer afraid for my life. The land around me seemed more pleasant, more like home. After six days of struggle and hardship, we had finally made it—and that was only the beginning.

Drug War Refugee

By: Brian Whitmer

"Another night of violence in the District," was basically how nearly every morning newscast during the summer and fall of 1992 in Washington, D.C., started. I ate breakfast each day that year while watching true-life scenes from the drug war being played out for me on videotape, a stream of arresting images in seemingly random order. It was chaotic and repetitious at the same time. I'd switch channels and get the same thing: "Another night of violence in the District." Different anchorman, same suit, same snazzy graphic of a chalk outline over his left shoulder. Then, with accompanying film footage of crying women and corpses under bloody sheets, a reporter would itemize the previous night's casualties and announce the cumulative body count. That was the year, you might recall, that Washington became as notorious for its homicide rate as for its political scheming. The whole metro area became known in the national news media as "The Murder Capital of the World," and from the attention we gave it locally, you'd think we were proud of the statistics. The words at the end of each report were just as predictable as the ones that began it: "Police have no leads or

suspects. Drugs are presumed the motive." That was the year I learned the term, "drive-by shooting." That was the year local junior high playgrounds became gunfight arenas. That was the year I decided to get out of town for a while.

I opted to spend Christmas and New Year's Day, not with family and friends, but with strangers in a distant land. I signed on as a student with a well-known outdoor leadership school which was running a course that holiday week on white-water canoeing and desert camping skills. The location of the course was southeastern Texas, in the barren yet starkly beautiful Chihuahuan Desert, not far from Big Bend National Park. The river, of course, was the Rio Grande.

My course in Texas began perfectly. The desert sun baked out much of the stress I'd been accumulating all year, and the desert air dried out the soggy, spongy moisture I'd soaked up from Washington's typical early winter drizzle. Before long, I felt as though I had truly "gotten away from it all." The turquoise sky remained clear for days on end; and on top of that, all my course-mates turned out to be swell folks. There were 10 of us in all: eight students and two instructors, Craig and Dave. We bonded right away and started having fun immediately. As much fun as we had, though, we always remained serious about a few key issues. For example, we didn't play around as much when it came to scouting and running rapids. The Rio was running terribly low that winter, and rocks that our instructors had never seen before were poking up everywhere as if craning their necks to watch us go by. Our boats were loaded down with gear, too, so we hit a lot of submerged stuff we couldn't see coming, and the canoes were prone to tip as the packs shifted around. Several of us took a couple of unanticipated swims early on, and, though, we and our gear came out mostly unharmed, we didn't like it very much. After that, it wasn't unusual for us to spend as long as 15 or 20 minutes scouting even the shortest of rapids from the safety of the shore.

One of the most exciting things for me about being on the Rio Grande was knowing that I was canoeing on the border between the United States and Mexico. I had never visited our southern neighbors before, and it felt kind of sneaky to dash over to their side every now and then to explore. In fact, the first thing I did when we put the boats in on the first day was to paddle over to the south bank of the river, pat the cliff wall affectionately, and shout, "Viva, Me-hi-co!" in a bad Spanish accent. My fellow students were amused, but I suspect Craig and Dave had heard that one before.

Unfortunately, there was also a dark side to our being on the border. The border, after all, is a source of conflict and controversy between the United States and Mexico, especially between our respective law enforcement agencies. A constant seepage of illicit narcotics and illegal immigrants permeates the border along its entire length. The United States, with its powerful economy, is an irresistible magnet pointed at Mexico, with its enormous population and its grinding poverty. A thin ribbon of river doesn't make a very effective barrier between two such giants. If it weren't for the vast desert, things would be far worse. As it is, the Border Patrol just barely keeps the lid on. Several times a day, my group was reminded of this grim situation by Border Patrol planes sweeping low over the canyons, checking us out. For the most part, though, our merry little band remained happily absorbed in the rigors of our course.

On the fifth day of the eight-day course, we found ourselves at the top of a nasty looking nest of rapids, the name of which I have forgotten or blocked from memory. My canoe partner that day, a beautiful young woman named Jenna, was an inexperienced paddler, but I trusted her abilities. More than that, I trusted her judgement. She was good at discriminating between the rapids she could handle and the ones it would be wiser to line the boat around. She was better at this than I, in fact, because she had her ego under control and didn't feel pressured to act foolishly macho. I admired this, even though I didn't emulate it.

Despite the minefield of obstacles in this swirly stretch of water, Jenna seemed powerfully attracted to the rapid. I think she judged it to be way up at the high end of our range of ability, but still within a reasonable margin of safety. I agreed, but we scouted the hell out of it just the same. So did our colleagues. Each pair of partners began conferring privately over a different section of water, picking their lines, plotting their strategies. After a while we'd regroup to confer with other pairs of partners. Then we'd all go back to the river again to rethink our choices. Ten minutes went by. Tension grew. No one moved toward the boats. Twenty minutes. Still we deliberated. If it was this tough to pick a line, we started to wonder, did we really have any business running the rapid? Thirty minutes passed. Finally, a couple of brave souls took to the water. While they steeled their hearts and girded their loins, Craig and Dave shot the rapid ahead of them and took up a position at the bottom, in the likelihood that they'd be needed down below to snatch up bodies and stray gear. We all watched their progress with intense interest, comparing their chosen path to the ones we'd considered. Some of us ooohhed. Some of us ahhhed. A few of us shrugged, unable to glean much without the benefit of a slow-motion replay.

"Let's watch 'em all," I whispered to Jenna, pulling her away from the boats. She nodded eagerly while the other sets of partners entreated each other to go next:

"After you."

"No, no. I insist."

"Really, it's no trouble at all ..."

Eventually, everyone was downstream except for me and Jenna, and we were still undecided about the best route to follow. By that time, we had probably been scouting the rapid for nearly 45 minutes.

It was then that the shots rang out.

No shit. Gunshots, right over our heads! It had to be smugglers. The river here was very narrow and easily accessible from both sides, yet it was sheltered from view by nearby foothills—a perfect site for clandestine crossings. I was nearly mesmerized by the sensation of adrenaline surging into my limbs, but then I was snapped back into alertness by two more cracks of gunfire.

I looked at Jenna. She looked at the wide open river, then back at me. I looked at some thick underbrush up the hill a few dozen yards, then back at Jenna. Nearly in a panic, I wondered which would be safer: hunkering down at the river bank under fairly good cover, or beating it out of there on the river with no cover at all? We didn't waste time debating it. Without a word exchanged between us, Jenna jumped in the front of the boat and I found myself pushing us off from the shore before she even had a chance to put paddle to water. We dropped to our knees and stroked furiously toward the rapid, trying to keep our heads down. I had just enough time before hitting the rapid to confirm that we'd probably made the right decision. After all, the shots seemed to have been fired over our heads, suggesting that what these banditos really wanted was for us to leave. And we were obliging as fast as we could!

I can't say that I remember much about running that particular rapid. I do remember thinking, *We can't afford to dump here!!* But everything else is mostly a blur. I don't even know if Jenna and I followed any of the lines we'd selected from shore. We were pretty much just making it up as we went careening down the chutes. Rocks would appear, and we'd avoid them. Haystacks would appear, and we'd crash them. A stroke here, a lean there and suddenly we were racing past our instructors. They had boldly waited at the bottom of the rapid and were now frantically waving us on to join the rest of the group, which had prudently moved well downstream already.

As Craig and Dave peeled into the current behind us, I stole a backward glance over my left shoulder and spotted the gunslingers. Not far up the hill from where Jenna and I had been scouting, two gringos on horseback rode jauntily down toward the river's edge. One had a rifle parked lazily on his shoulder; the other was pointing at us. Both were laughing at our frenzied departure.

We ate a very late lunch that day many miles downstream from the free-fire zone. As we discussed that morning's adventure over peanut butter and bagels, we concluded that we must have been scouting at a prearranged drop site where smugglers bringing up drugs from Mexico intended to rendezvous with other smugglers bringing down cash from the United States. Perhaps the American crooks felt that our presence at the rapid might deter their Hispanic associates and sour the deal. Then again, perhaps they just needed a break from the tedium of awaiting the drop. Either way, they dispatched us handily by the most persuasive means at their disposal.

While I chugged down half a bottle of water, Jenna joked to the group that I should be looking forward to getting back to Washington, D.C. "He'll probably feel safer in 'The Murder Capital of the World,' " she chuckled, "than out here in the lawless wilderness." At first, we all laughed in agreement. But then I sobered up, realizing that what we had witnessed on the river a few short hours ago was merely another link in an immense distribution chain in a global black market. The shipment of drugs we had just watched come over the border—and all the violence that normally accompanies such deadly cargo—would probably be on the streets of the District by the time I got home. I chewed on that for a while.

"Hey!" said Dave suddenly. "Happy New Year, everybody!" He was trying to sound chipper but couldn't quite mask the irony in his voice.

"Oh yeah," said someone softly, almost mournfully. "I guess it's New Year's Day, isn't it?"

For several minutes no one spoke. We just shuffled our feet a little and smiled somewhat grimly at one another.

An enigmatic poet named Jim Harrison once wrote that sometimes the only answer to death is lunch, so I slumped down on a nearby rock, finished off my bottle of water and dipped another bagel in the peanut butter.

Appendix

Author Biographies

CHAD LEDUC

Chad LeDuc was born on the prairies of western North Dakota on April Fool's Day 1954, and maintains a standing cash offer to anyone who can tell him a joke about being born on that day and in that place that he hasn't heard before. He grew up in Minot and did seven years hard time at the University of North Dakota studying wildlife and law, in that order, before moving to the Rainy Lake region of Minnesota commonly known, of course, as "God's Country." He lives there with his patient wife, Brenda, his loving kids, Jaime and Charlie, and their 15 or so howling sled dogs. He enjoys all the amenities of the outdoors but also finds time to practice law with his sometimes understanding partners in what is reputed to be the finest four-lawyer law firm north of the Mississippi in Koochiching County.

MATT AKERS HUDSON

Matt Akers Hudson is an outdoor educator based in Tempe, Arizona. He is currently pursuing a master's degree in outdoor/experiential education at Prescott College. In addition to his studies, he works as a climbing guide, rafting guide, challenge-course facilitator and part-time college instructor. He was formerly the editor of *The Outdoor Network*, a quarterly publication for Outdoor Education professionals.

MICHAEL SHEPHERD

I grew up hunting and fishing the very wetlands described in Old Rocksalt, and the story is loosely based on truth—how loosely, I'll never confess. Placing in the "No Shit" contest brought a full backpack of sunshine into this windowless dungeon that holds me. I am confined in Pelican Bay State

Prison's Security Housing Unit (SHU) for manslaughter. When I wasn't enjoying the outdoors on foot, I rode a Harley. Some of the watering holes I rode into got a mite wild and, well, shit happens. The SHU is a supermax prison where prisoners see nothing of the outside world. I've seen real trees, real earth and have felt unfiltered sunshine only twice in the last three-and-a-half years. Writing has become my means of escape. I've been published once before by *Outlaw Biker* magazine. Being published by ICS Books, Inc. has sharpened my drive to pursue writing seriously, and I'll be there for next year's "No Shit" contest. Look out John Long, I'm comin' after that number one spot.

ANDRE THEISEN

Andre Theisen has pointy eyebrows and pairs his socks according to weight rather than color. He has been a bartender, a camp counselor, a tour guide, a temp slave and a teacher. He has taught in the South Bronx, in northern Japan and on a Missouri commune. He helps direct a summer camp in northern Minnesota. He isn't convinced the earth would be knocked out of its orbit if everyone in China jumped simultaneously, but he sure would like them to give it a try.

BUCK TILTON

Buck Tilton has been chained to the directorship of the Wilderness Medicine Institute in Pitkin, Colorado, far too long. Away from the Institute, when not fishing, paddling, backpacking or trying other equally important pursuits, he rots his mind by writing. As a contributing editor for *Backpacker* and a freelancer to several other mags, he has had more than 500 articles published. His name appears on the cover of 12 books including at least two which indicate his need to do more fishing and paddling: *Sex in the Outdoors* and *How to Die in the Outdoors*, both printed with embarrassment by ICS Books, Inc.

BRIAN WHITMER

Brian Whitmer, 35, teaches American history and world studies in Silver Spring, Maryland. His summers and holidays are divided between working for Outward Bound and making various other excursions into the wilderness in search of adventure. More often than not, he finds it. Brian is working on a compilation of essays which re-examine America's past from the sidelong perspective of an avid outdoorsman and history buff.

MARK DEEM

A self-proclaimed "professional amateur," Mark Deem lives in San Francisco. Kayaking seas and rivers, climbing rock and ice, skiing, snowboarding, mountaineering, trekking, diving, rafting, surfing, mountain biking and biomedical engineering occupy his misadventures. "Malay Melee" and "Slammed on the Salmon" are his first published stories. Deem would like to thank his partner, Dave, for trying so often to kill him.

TED GEARING

At the age of 13, Ted Gearing built a boat out of wood salvaged from an old tree house and launched it upon the turgid waters of the family pond. Horses, cows and fish collapsed with laughter as he and his craft sank slowly out of sight. Since then, he's amassed a fleet of 12 canoes and kayaks, all of which he has managed to sink at one time or another ... hard on the reputation, but it makes for interesting stories. Gearing lives with his wife, Cathie, on the banks of the Finley River in southwest Missouri. His articles have appeared in *Paddler.*

KIPP CAMPBELL

Kipp Campbell received his Masters of Social Work degree from Wilfred Laurier University. He has worked in Psychiatry, Addictions and Family Services. His orientation is family treatment with a strong emphasis on community involvement, believing that it is necessary to be both a treatment person and an agent for change. He has been a field instructor for numerous universities in Canada and the United States and has served on the Metro Toronto District Health Council. Kipp is a recipient of the Commemorative Medal for the 125th Anniversary of Canadian Confederation. He serves as the executive director of The Intersect Youth and Family Services Society in Prince George, British Columbia. Kipp reports that he has climbed 5.10c and has only been climbing for two years. Since moving to Prince George from Toronto, Kipp has sealed his climbing and mountaineering fate (and doubtless more "No Shit" experiences) by helping to organize a chapter of the Alpine Club of Canada, now boasting more than 60 members.

MARY BEDINGFIELDSMITH

Mary Bedingfieldsmith lives in Utah's Cache Valley. She shares her home with one well-mannered, housebroken cat and Scott, her not-so housebroken husband. In real life, she teaches sixth graders, but when she's not teaching, she bakes a mean loaf of bread, reads, runs and trains llamas to be housebroken (she's not kidding). Mary would spend all of her time doing perfectly "normal" things if it weren't for the fact that Scott is a photographer who needs a key grip. That means she gets to follow Scott all over the bloody countryside looking for photos. Often they find themselves in the middle of a crazy situation—fodder for an equally wild story. If the two of them ever grow up, they hope to live far away from cities, raise llamas, grow a big garden and continue adventuring.

JOHN LONG

John Long's instructional books have made him a best-seller in the outdoor industry, and his award-winning stories—known for taut action and psychological intensity—have been widely anthologized and translated into many languages. His current literary fiction has appeared in everything from *Granta* to *Reader's Digest*. Of his 12 books, more than 750,000 copies are currently in print. A legendary performer in rock climbing and adventuring, Long made the first one-day ascent of El Capitan, and the first free ascent of Washington Column's East Face (both in Yosemite Valley), still considered the world's greatest free climb. Notable expeditions include: Baffin Island-North Pole; first coast-to-coast traverse of Borneo; discovery and exploration of the world's largest river cave (Gulf Province, Papua, New Guinea); first descent, Angel Falls, Venezuela; and first land crossing of Indonesian New Guinea (Irian Jaya), said to be the most primitive region in the world. From the late '70s through the '80s, Long wrote for various network television shows. His novella, *Rogue's Babylon*, was carved apart and reassembled in the Sylvester Stallone movie, *Cliffhanger*. One-eighth Comanche, Long has been deeply interested in all aspects of Native American culture for many years, a voyage of self-discovery that resulted in his recently published anthology of Indian folklore and legends, *Pale Moon*. Long, winner of first place in the "No Shit" contest last year and then again this year has agreed (after being threatened with a darn good thrashing) not to enter next year.

D.V. TYLER

D.V. Tyler spent 10 years in radio and television broadcasting in Los Angeles, Hong Kong and Hawaii. For the past 30 years, Tyler has owned a state-of-the-art recording and video post-production studio in Honolulu. He has skied Mauna Kea, hiked Aleyska, kayaked the Rogue, surfed Waikiki, dived Fiji and claims to be very tired. At the time this is being published, Tyler is hoping to be tramping around the interior of the Haleakala volcano on Maui. With luck, the volcano will remain dormant.

ANTHONY RICHARDS

Anthony Richards makes his home in Nova Scotia, Canada, with his dancer/choreographer wife. He is a professor at Dalhousie University where he teaches adventure-based experiential learning.

BILL CROSS

Bill Cross is a writer and river runner living in Ashland, Oregon. He is a co-author, with Jim Cassady and Fryar Calhoun, of *Western Whitewater from the Rockies to the Pacific: A River Guide for Raft, Kayak and Canoe*, which covers some 165 rivers in 11 western states. Bill's adventures and misadventures on western rivers have inspired articles for *Adventure West, Canoe & Kayak, Outdoor Family* and other publications, and he is a contributing editor for *Paddler Magazine*. He runs rivers with his wife and three children, and occasionally brings along an ancient springer spaniel for added challenge.

DAVID SCOTT

David Scott has been interested in wilderness living since he first stepped into the woods. Although he is only 24, his interests have taken him around the globe in search of the spirit of adventure. He has camped and stayed "everywhere he could" from wilderness areas in the United States and Canada to remote areas of China, learning and honing his skills from the people he has met along the way. Scott is also a musician, songwriter, poet, pilot, rustic furniture builder and a lecturer for such diverse groups as kindergartners to the Wilderness Medical Society. He is also author of *Camping's Little Book of Wisdom*, and the full story of this adventure, *Paradise Creek*, both published by ICS Books, Inc.

SCOTT WHITMIRE

Scott Whitmire has been a member of the California Smokejumpers for nine years, six of which he has been an instructor. In that time, he has amassed more than 160 jumps, with only three actual tree landings ... so far. Whitmire has fought fires for the Forest Service for more than 14 seasons, and hopes to develop his writing and photography skills enough to enable him to freelance full time. Whitmire grew up in the Sierra Nevada foothills near Fresno, and cultivated his love for the outdoors through hiking, working and playing in the mountains. Whitmire is currently the Sports Editor for the Shasta College newspaper, and covers sports for a small weekly publication in Redding, California.

BROUGHTON COBURN

Broughton Coburn lived in Nepal and the Himalayas more than 17 years, overseeing wildlife conservation efforts for the United Nations, World Wildlife Fund and other agencies. His first book, *Nepali Aama: Portrait of a Nepalese Hill Woman*, a photo-documentary of the life of an elder of the Gurung tribe, was first published in 1982, and was awarded the Washington State Governor's Writer's Day award. More recently, Coburn and his wife, Didi, took Aama, at age 84, on a 12,000-mile pilgrimage in search of the soul of the United States. In May 1995, Anchor Books published *Aama in America: A Pilgrimage of the Heart*. Coburn graduated from Harvard College in 1973, and now lives in Jackson Hole, Wyoming.

PAUL SUWALSKI

Paul Suwalski has made a career in the great outdoors. For the past 17 summers, Paul has been the head guide for the Lane Guest Ranch near Estes Park, Colorado. He has made four trips to the Antarctic where he has worked in logistics for the science community. He has spent several winters in both Vail and Aspen, perfecting the telemark turn. Paul enjoys writing, photography and throwing tennis balls for his two neurotic labs.

LORRIE PARKER

Lorrie Kidwell Parker is a proud eccentric "girl" who was born and bred (and still living and laughing) in West Virginia. She started writing poetry around the age of thirteen, as a way of dealing with her anger at having to run through life's seemingly unfair and confusing "obstacle course". She came upon the writings of Lewis Grizzard, Erma Bombeck, (and a few issues of National Lampoon) and realized she'd be alright being different. She knows for sure that the pen is mightier than the sword (She can barely afford to buy the sickle she uses to cut her grass, much less a sword!). Bic pens are her chosen weapon. She has a high school education, a membership in the Tri-State Writer's Guild, and a damn strong desire to keep on writing. Her two children, two grandsons, three dogs, and four cats are proud of her. Her iguana doesn't seem to care one way or the other.

Judging Criteria

All stories published within this book were presented to the judges anonymously and were submitted in the same format and style in which the contestants submitted them to us (if we received a hard-to-read copy with sloppy editing, that is what went to the judges). The judges were asked to evaluate and score each story in two categories: Entertainment Value / Compelling Storyline and Professional Crafting / Writing Quality. Each category was awarded a point total between 1 and 50, with one being the least favorable and 50 representing writing perfection (no, no one earned a 50, but yes, a few came close). Both scores were then totaled and each story was awarded an overall score somewhere between 2 and 100. I tallied the scores from each of the three judges to arrive at each story's final score. I congratulate all the finalists and the top 23 finishers whose stories appear in this book.

The judging panel involved editors and publishers from the following magazines:

Climbing — Michael Kennedy, editor and publisher

Canoe & Kayak — Judy Harrison, publisher; David Harrison, editor-in-chief

Women's Sports and Fitness — Jane McConnell, publisher and editor-in-chief

A very special thanks to all the judges from myself and ICS Books.

IT'S TIME FOR
ANOTHER BOOK ...and
another writing contest!

3rd Annual "NO SHIT!
THERE I WAS"... Contest

Award-winning author and humorist Michael Hodgson and ICS Books are seeking your accounts of personal "No shit, there I was ..." stories. Tell us your best outdoor adventure tale of glory relating to climbing, mountaineering, scuba diving, skiing, whitewater boating, mountain biking, hang gliding, adventure travel—the list is endless as long as it pertains to the outdoors (no urban assault or my dog ate the cat stories please). Stories that may put the author at personal risk of embarrassment or international incident (such as the imbibing of local intoxicants while traveling abroad and/or sex-related fables—nothing illegal that will get us all into trouble please) may be published under a pen name at the author's request. If your story is good enough, it may be published along with a select number of other top story entries in Michael Hodgson's and ICS Books' upcoming title, "No Shit! There I Was ... !" If your story is really good, and we mean embellished with appropriate humor and bravado, combined with a touch of believable exaggeration, you may be awarded $2,000 as the winner of Michael Hodgson's and ICS Books' third annual "No Shit! There I Was..." contest. Runner up wins $500. While this may not be the quickest path to fame and fortune, seeing your story in print sure as heck promises to be a lot of fun and who knows, Hollywood may seek the rights to your story—nahhh!

Send two copies of your story in double-spaced, typewritten form enclosed with a signed copy and an official entry form to ICS Books. One copy of your entry must be ready for judging with all author identifying marks removed and only the title of the work and page numbers at the top of each page. All entries must be received by December 1, 1995. Winner and runner up of the contest will be announced August 1996 during *Outdoor Retailer's* Summer Market in Salt Lake City. All authors of stories selected for publication will receive an autographed copy of "No Shit! There I Was ..." Submission of story for contest grants one-time rights and permission to Michael Hodgson and ICS Books to publish your story in "No Shit! There I Was ..." and subsequent promotional material with only byline attribution and no financial compensation. Contest is not open to ICS Books employees. Judges of the final round of the contest include a select panel of top magazine editors. Preliminary qualification judging to pare the field down to a final round of maximum of fifty stories is performed by a select panel of professional guides, Michael Hodgson and Tom Todd, publisher of ICS Books. Decision of the judges is final.

Of course, no one can enter without an official entry form. To request your entry form, contest deadline information and prize details, either call ICS Books at 219 769-0585, fax ICS at 219 769-6085, or write ICS at 1370 East 86th Place, Merrillville, IN. 46410.

Statement Regarding Acquisition of Rights

Author Michael Hodgson and ICS Books only seek to acquire one-time rights for publication of contest entrant's stories in "No Shit, There I Was" ... (any edition)! Any and all contest entrants may subsequently sell their stories to magazines, newspapers or other publications at will. Previously published stories will also be considered. Any request for reprints from the book that involve a contestant's story will be referred directly to the contestant for negotiation.

if it ain't fun, forget it!

No Shit There I Was. . .   Vol. 1
wild stories from wild people
Edited by Michael Hodgson
It all started out as a reckless but innocent ritual of
some western raft guides. Tales so adventure
packed and hyperbolic that they could rarely be
completely believed.
192 pages 6x9 Illustrated
ISBN 0-934802-97-1   **$11.99**

Sex in the Outdoors
A humorous approach to recreation
by Robert Rose, M.D. and Buck Tilton
"A tremendously funny read."
-Adventure West, Spring '94
"A rather humorous romp."
-Detroit News
96 pages 6x9 paperback
ISBN 0-934802-86-6   **$6.99**

*Explore the Outdoors safely and
comfortably with*

The Basic Essentials Series

• Inexpensive
• Latest Techniques
• Abundantly Illustrated
• 72 Pages of Unique Advice

$5.99 Each

P.O. Box 10767 Merrillville, IN 46410
1-800-541-7323 • fax 1-800-336-8334

Available at these fine stores: **EREHWON, L.L. BEAN, REI, EMS, HUDSON TRAIL,**
A-16, SPORT CHALET, GALYANS, BOARDERS
and your favorite bookstore or outdoor outlet.
For a complete catalog call ICS BOOKS TOLL FREE AT 1-800-541-7323

Discover a New Point of View

No matter where you're headed, Women's Sports & Fitness magazine gets you where you want to go. Packed with clear information, tips and techniques that will help you reach your personal fitness goals, every issue of WS&F features:

✓ Sensible health advice
✓ Nutritional know-how
✓ Ways to avoid injury–and treat the injuries you have
✓ Fitness vacation information
✓ Reviews of the best new gear
✓ Effective training tips and techniques
✓ Profiles of ordinary women doing extraordinary things
✓ Inspiration and advice that will keep you going day after day!

For fastest service, call 1-800-877-5281. Or just clip this coupon and send it to Women's Sports & Fitness, P.O. Box 472 Mt. Morris, IL 61054-9908

WOMEN'S SPORTS & FITNESS MAGAZINE

☐ **Yes!** Enter my subscription to Women's Sports & Fitness magazine. Bill me later.

1 year–8 issues–$12.98 (plus $1.99 delivery)

Name _____
    (first)   (last)
Address _____ Apt. # _____

City _____ State _____ Zip _____

Foreign orders: add $20 per subscription per year prepaid in U.S. funds only. Canadian orders: add $9 per subscription per year. One year basic subscription: $19.97.
Women's Sports & Fitness, P.O. Box 472
Mt. Morris, IL 61054-9908
A3ANST   Printed in U.S.A.

Whatever *YOUR* Paddling Pleasure...
Canoeing or Kayaking,

calm-water touring, wilderness trips or the
rush of whitewater...you can be there all
year long in the pages of CANOE magazine
THE #1 RESOURCE FOR CANOEING AND
KAYAKING.

For 20 Years, CANOE magazine, the award
winning publication has been the most complete
resource for canoeing and kayaking and the entire
range of paddlesports. The where-to-go, what-to-take,
and how-to-use-it paddling magazine of the 90's.

SUBSCRIBE TODAY...Save 50% off the cover price!
Special Introductory Offer 1 year (6 issues) for $11.97

CALL 1-800 MY CANOE (1-800-692-2663) WE WILL BILL YOU LATER. If for any
reason you are not satisfied with your very first copy of CANOE magazine, simply write
cancel on your bill and return same to us...**Take a look at *CANOE*, without risk
or obligation.** CALL TODAY! *CANOE* MAGAZINE, P. O. BOX 3146, KIRKLAND,
WA 98083-3146.

Please allow 4 to 6 weeks for delivery of your first copy. Add $3 per year for Canadian
subscriptions. Other foreign subscriptions are $36 per year (airmail) pre-paid in US funds.

*   *   *   *   *   *   *

**DEALER INQUIRIES WELCOME! *CANOE* MAGAZINE has a
profitable program for you. Join our <u>Retailer Network</u>, increase your
profits, and receive many benefits. For more information, Please call
our toll free line...1-800 MY CANOE (1-800-692-2663) or 206-827-6363.
CANOE Magazine, P. O. Box 3146, Kirkland, WA 98083-3146.**

*   *   *   *   *   *   *

"CONGRATULATIONS" TO ALL THE WINNERS WHOSE STORIES APPEAR IN
THIS BOOK. Judy Harrison, Publisher, *CANOE* Magazine was honored to be chosen
as one of the judges to read and evaluate the 22 stories selected as finals for print in
this book. We, especially "SALUTE" the First Place, and First Runner-up winners!

*Celebrating 25 years of covering
the vertical world like no one else.
Experience...*

CLIMBING

INSPIRED   INTENSE   INFORMATIVE   INVOLVED

The anxiety of climbing Cerro Torre was momentarily replaced by an equally intense sense of exhilaration and comfort.

— DAN CAUTHORN
THE WILD WILD WEST FACE OF CERRO TORRE
APRIL/MAY 1993

It was the shadow that had first caught my eye. As a climber, I was attuned to the nature of shadows. They reveal the subtle overhangs, cracks and dihedrals in a rock; therefore, shadows can be climbed. I pulled a piton off my rack and drove it deeply into the shadow.

— DUANE RALEIGH
A STONE'S THROW
AUGUST/SEPTEMBER 1990

In order to climb properly on a big peak one must free oneself of fear. This means you must write yourself off before any big climb. You must say to yourself, "I may die here."

— DOUG SCOTT
QUOTED BY GREG CHILD IN SEEKING THE BALANCE
FEBRUARY/MARCH 1989

SUBSCRIPTIONS: $28 FOR ONE YEAR (8 ISSUES) OR $48 FOR TWO YEARS (16 ISSUES). TO ORDER, SEND YOUR CHECK TO CLIMBING, 1101 VILLAGE ROAD, SUITE LLB1, CARBONDALE, COLORADO 81623. FOR FAST CREDIT CARD ORDERS, CALL US AT (970) 963-9449; FAX: (970) 963-9442.